Conversation:

Its Faults and Its Graces

By

Andrew Preston Peabody

Young Ladies,

You have made me happy by your kind invitation to meet you, and to address you on this anniversary. A day spent in this room at your annual examination, nearly two years ago, was a season of privilege and enjoyment not readily to be forgotten. I had previously entertained a high regard for your instructor. I then learned to know him by his work; and, were he not here, I should be glad to extend beyond a single sentence my congratulations with you that you are his pupils.

I have said that I accepted your invitation with gladness. Yet, in preparing myself to meet you, I find a degree of embarrassment. This is for you a season of recreation,—a high festival; and I am accustomed to use my pen and voice only on grave occasions, and for solemn services. I know not how to add to your amusement. Should I undertake to make sport for you, my awkwardness would give you more mirth than my wit. The best that I can do is to select some subject that is or ought to be interesting to you, and to endeavor to blend a little instruction with the gayer and more lively notes of the occasion. The lesson shall be neither tediously long nor needlessly grave.

I propose to offer you a few hints on *conversation*. How large a portion of life does it fill up! How innumerable are its ministries and its uses! It is the most refined species of recreation,—the most sparkling source of merriment. It interweaves with a never-resting shuttle the bonds of domestic sympathy. It fastens the ties of friendship, and runs along the golden links of the chain of love. It enriches charity, and makes the gift twice blessed.

There is, perhaps, a peculiar appropriateness in the selection of this topic for an address to young ladies; for they do more than any other class in the community towards establishing the general tone and standard of social intercourse. The voices of many of you already, I doubt not, strike the key-note of home conversation; and you are fast approaching an age when you will take prominent places in general society; will be the objects of peculiar regard; and will, in a great measure, determine whether the social converse in your respective circles shall be vulgar or refined, censorious or kindly, frivolous or dignified. It was said by a wise man of antiquity,—"Only give me the making of songs for the people, and I care not who makes the laws." In our unmusical age and land, talking occupies the place which songs did among the melody-loving Greeks; and he who could tune the many-voiced harp of the social party, need crave no higher office or more potent sway.

Permit me now to enumerate some of the characteristics of graceful, elegant, and profitable conversation, commencing with the lower graces, and passing on to the higher.

Let me first beg you, if you would be good talkers, to form and fix now, (for you can do this only now,) habits of correct and easy pronunciation. The words which you now miscall, it will cost you great pains in after life to pronounce aright, and you will always be in danger of returning inadvertently to your old pronunciation. There are two extremes which you ought equally to shun. One is that of carelessness; the other, that of extreme precision, as if the sound of the words uttered were constantly uppermost in the mind. This last fault always suggests the idea of vanity and pedantry, and is of itself enough to add a deep indigo hue to a young lady's reputation.

One great fault of New England pronunciation is, that the work is performed too much by the outer organs of speech. The tones of the voice have but little depth. Instead of a generous play of the throat and lungs, the throat almost closes, and the voice seems to be formed in the mouth. It is this that gives what is called a *nasal* tone to the voice, which, when denied free range through its lawful avenues, rushes in part through the nose. We notice the nasal pronunciation in excess here and there in an individual, while Englishmen and Southerners observe it as a prevailing characteristic of all classes of people in the Northern States. Southerners in general are much less careful and accurate in pronunciation than we are; but they more than compensate for this deficiency by the full, round tones in which they utter themselves. In our superficial use of the organs of speech, there are some consonants which we are prone to omit altogether. This is especially the case with *g* in words that end with *ing*. Nine persons out of ten say *singin* instead of *singing*. I know some public speakers, and many private ones, who never pronounce the *t* in such words as *object* and *prospect*. Very few persons give the right sound to *r* final. *Far* is generally pronounced as if it were written *fah*. Now, I would not have the full Hibernian roll of the *r;* but I would have the presence of the letter more distinctly recognized, than it often is, even by persons of refined and fastidious taste.

Let me next beg you to shun all the ungrammatical vulgarisms which are often heard, but which never fail to grate harshly on a well-tuned ear. If you permit yourselves to use them now, you will never get rid of them. I know a venerable and accomplished lawyer, who has stood at the head of his profession in this State, and has moved in the most refined society for half a century, who to this day says *haint* for *has not*, having acquired the habit when a schoolboy. I have known persons who have for years tried unsuccessfully to break themselves of saying *done* for *did*, and *you and I* for *you and me*. Many well-educated persons, through the power of long habit, persist in saying *shew* for *showed*, while they know perfectly well that they might, with equal propriety, substitute *snew* for *snowed;* and there is not far hence a clergyman, marvellously precise and fastidious in his choice of words, who is very apt to commence his sermon by saying, "I *shew* you in a recent discourse." A false delicacy has very generally introduced *drank* as the perfect participle of *drink*, instead of *drunk*, which alone has any respectable authority in its favor; and the imperfect tense and perfect participle have been similarly confounded in many other cases. I know not what grammar you use in this school. I trust that it is an old one; for some of the new grammars sanction these vulgarisms, and in looking over their tables of irregular verbs, I have sometimes half expected to have the book dashed from my hand by the indignant ghost of Lindley Murray. Great care and discretion should be employed in the use of the common abbreviations of the negative forms of the substantive and auxiliary verbs. *Can't, don't,* and *haven't,* are admissible in rapid conversation on trivial subjects. *Isn't* and *hasn't* are more harsh, yet tolerated by respectable usage. *Didn't, couldn't, wouldn't,* and *shouldn't,* make as unpleasant combinations of consonants as can well be uttered, and fall short but by one remove of those unutterable names of Polish gentlemen which sometimes excite our wonder in the columns of a newspaper. *Won't* for *will not,* and *aint* for *is not* or *are not,* are absolutely vulgar; and *aint,* for *has not* or *have not,* is utterly intolerable.

Nearly akin to these offences against good grammar is another untasteful practice, into which you are probably more in danger of falling, and which is a crying sin among young ladies,—I mean the use of exaggerated, extravagant forms of speech,—saying *splendid* for *pretty, magnificent* for *handsome, horrid* for *very, horrible* for *unpleasant, immense* for *large, thousands* or *myriads* for any number greater than *two.* Were I to write down, for one day, the conversation of some young ladies of my acquaintance, and then to interpret it literally, it would imply that, within the compass of twelve or fourteen hours, they had met with more marvellous adventures and hair-breadth escapes, had passed through more distressing experiences, had seen more imposing spectacles, had endured more fright, and enjoyed more rapture, than would suffice for half a dozen common lives. This habit is attended with many inconveniences. It deprives you of the intelligible use of strong expressions when you need them. If you use them all the time, nobody understands or believes you when you use them in earnest. You are in the same predicament with the boy who cried WOLF so often, when there was no wolf, that nobody would go to his relief when the wolf came. This habit has also a very bad moral bearing. Our words have a reflex influence upon our characters. Exaggerated speech makes one careless of the truth. The habit of using words without regard to their rightful meaning, often leads one to distort facts, to misreport conversations, and to magnify statements, in matters in which the literal truth is important to be told. You can never trust the testimony of one who in common conversation is indifferent to the import, and regardless of the power, of words. I am acquainted with persons whose representations of facts always need translation and correction, and who have utterly lost their reputation for veracity, solely through this habit of overstrained and extravagant speech. They do not mean to lie; but they have a dialect of their own, in which words bear an entirely different sense from that given to them in the daily intercourse of discreet and sober people.

In this connection, it may not be amiss to notice a certain class of phrases, often employed to fill out and dilute sentences, such as, *I'm sure,—I declare,—That's a fact,—You know,—I want to know,—Did you ever?—Well! I never,*—and the like. All these forms of speech disfigure conversation, weaken the force of the assertions or statements with which they are connected, and give unfavorable impressions as to the good breeding of the person that uses them.

You will be surprised, young ladies, to hear me add to these counsels, —"Above all things, swear not at all." Yet there is a great deal of swearing among those who would shudder at the very thought of being profane. The Jews, who were afraid to use the most sacred names in common speech, were accustomed to swear by the temple, by the altar, and by their own heads; and these oaths were rebuked and forbidden by divine authority. I know not why the rebuke and prohibition apply not with full force to the numerous oaths by *goodness, faith, patience,* and *mercy,* which we hear from lips that mean to be neither coarse nor irreverent, in the schoolroom, street, and parlor; and a moment's reflection will convince any well-disposed person, that, in the exclamation *Lor,* the cutting off of a single letter from a consecrated word can hardly save one from the censure and the penalty written in the third commandment. I do not regard these expressions as harmless. I believe them inconsistent with Christian laws of speech. Nor do they accord with the simple, quiet habit of mind and tone of feeling which are the most favorable to happiness and usefulness, and which sit as gracefully on gay and buoyant youth as on the sedateness of maturer years. The frame of mind in which a young lady says, in reply to a question, *Mercy! no,* is very different from that which prompts the simple, modest *no.* Were there any room for doubt, I should have some doubt of the truth of the former answer; for the unnatural, excited, fluttered state of mind implied in the use of the oath, might indicate either an unfitness to weigh the truth, or an unwillingness to acknowledge it.

In fine, transparency is an essential attribute of all graceful and becoming speech. Language ought to represent the speaker's ideas, and neither more nor less. Exclamations, needless expletives, unmeaning extravagances, are as untasteful as the streamers of tattered finery which you sometimes see fluttering about the person of a dilapidated belle. Let your thoughts be as strong, as witty, as brilliant, as you can make them; but never seek to atone for feeble thought by large words, or to rig out foolish conceits in the spangled robe of genuine wit. Speak as you think and feel; and let the tongue always be an honest interpreter to the heart.

But it is time that we passed to higher considerations. There are great laws of duty and religion which should govern our conversation; and the divine Teacher assures us that even for our idle words we are accountable to Him who has given us the power of speech. Now, I by no means believe that there is any principle of our religion which frowns upon wit or merriment, or forbids playful speech at fit seasons and within due limits. The very fact that the Almighty has created the muscles which produce the smile and the laugh, is a perpetual rebuke to those who would call all laughter madness, and all mirth folly. Amusement, in its time and place, is a great good; and I know of no amusement so refined, so worthy an intellectual being, as that conversation which is witty and still kind, playful, yet always reverent, which recreates from toil and care, but leaves no sting, and violates no principle of brotherly love or religious duty.

Evil speaking, slander, detraction, gossip, scandal, are different names for one of the chief dangers to be guarded against in conversation; and you are doing much towards defending yourselves against it by the generous mental culture which you enjoy in this seminary. The demon of slander loves an empty house. A taste for scandal betrays a vacant mind. Furnish your minds, then, by useful reading and study, and by habits of reflection and mental industry, that you may be able to talk about subjects as well as about people,—about events too long past or too remote to be interwoven with slander. But, if you must talk about people, why not about their good traits and deeds? The truest ingenuity is that which brings hidden excellences to light; for virtue is in her very nature modest and retiring, while faults lie on the surface and are detected with half an eye.

You will undoubtedly be careful to have your words always just and kind, if you will only take a sufficiently thorough view of the influence of your habits of conversation, both in the formation of your own characters and in determining the happiness of others. But how low an estimate do many of us make of the power of the tongue! How little account we are apt to take of our words! Have we not all at times said to ourselves, "Oh! it is only a word!" when it may have been sharp as a drawn sword, have given more pain than a score of blows, and done more harm than our hands could have wrought in a month? Why is it that the slanderer and the tale-bearer regard themselves as honest and worthy people, instead of feeling that they are accursed of God and man? It is because they deal in evil words only, and they consider words as mere nought. Why is it that the carping tongue, which filches a little from everybody's good name, can hardly utter itself without a sneer, and makes every fair character its prey, thinks better of itself than a petty pilferer would? It is because by long, though baseless prescription, the tongue has claimed for itself a license denied to every other member and faculty.

But, in point of fact, your words not only express, but help create, your characters. Speech gives definiteness and permanence to your thoughts and feelings. The unuttered thought may fade from the memory,—may be chased away by better thoughts,—may, indeed, hardly be a part of your own mind; for, if suggested from without, and met without a welcome, and with disapproval and resistance, it is not yours. But by speech you adopt thoughts, and the voice that utters them is as a pen that engraves them indelibly on the soul. If you can suppress unkind thoughts, so that, when they rise in your breast, and mount to your very lips, you leave them unuttered, you are not on the whole unkind,—your better nature has the supremacy. But if these wrong feelings often find utterance, though you call it hasty utterance, there is reason to fear that they flow from a bitter fountain within.

Consider, also, how large a portion speech makes up of the lives of all. It occupies the greater part of the waking hours of many of us; while express acts of a moral bearing, compared with our words, are rare and few. Indeed, in many departments of duty, words are our only possible deeds,—it is by words alone that we can perform or violate our duty. Many of the most important forms of charity are those of speech. Alms-giving is almost the only expression of charity of which the voice is not the chief minister; and alms, conferred in silent coldness, or with chiding or disdainful speech, freeze the spirit, though they may warm the body. Speech, too, is the sole medium of a countless host of domestic duties and observances. There are, indeed, in every community many whose only activity seems to be in words. There are many young ladies, released from the restraints of school, and many older ladies, with few or no domestic burdens, with no worldly avocation and no taste for reading, whose whole waking life, either at their own homes or from house to house, is given to the exercise, for good or evil, of the tongue,—that unruly member. And how blessed might they make that exercise,—for how many holy ministries of love, sympathy, and charity might it suffice,—how many wounds might it prevent or heal,—did they only believe and feel that they were writing out their own characters in their daily speech! But too many of them forget this. So long as they do not knowingly and absolutely lie, they feel no responsibility for their words. They deem themselves virtuous, because they refrain from vices to which they have not the shadow of a temptation; but carp, backbite, and carry ill reports from house to house, with an apostle's zeal and a martyr's devotedness. To say nothing of the social effect of such a life, is not the tongue thus employed working out spiritual death for the soul in whose service it is busy? I know of no images too vile to portray such a character. The dissection of a slanderer's or talebearer's heart would present the most loathsome specimen of morbid anatomy conceivable. It is full of the most malignant poison. Its life is all mean, low, serpent-like,—a life that cannot bear the light, but finds all its nourishment and growth in darkness. Were these foul and odious forms of speech incapable of harming others,—did human reptiles of this class creep about in some outward guise, in which they could be recognized by all, and their words be taken for what they are worth, and no more,—still I would beg them, for their own sakes, not to degrade God's image, in which they were created, into the likeness of a creeping thing; I would entreat them not to be guilty of the meanest and most miserable of all forms of spiritual suicide; I would beseech them, if they are determined to sell their souls, to get some better price for them than the scorn and dread of all whose esteem is worth having.

In this connection, we ought to take into account the very large class of literally idle words. How many talk on unthinkingly and heedlessly, as if the swift exercise of the organs of speech were the great end of life! The most trivial news of the day, the concerns of the neighborhood, the floating gossip, whether good-natured or malignant, dress, food, frivolous surmises, paltry plans, vanities too light to remain an hour upon the memory,—these are the sole staple of what too many call conversation; and many are the young people who are training themselves in the use of speech for no higher or better purpose. But such persons have the threatened judgment visibly following their idle speech. Their minds grow superficial and shallow. They constantly lose ground, if they ever had any, as intellectual and moral beings. Such speech makes a person, of however genteel training, coarse and vulgar, and that not only in character, but even in voice and manners, and with sad frequency it obliterates traits of rich loveliness and promise. The merely idle tongue is also very readily betrayed into overt guilt. One cannot indulge in idle, reckless talk, without being implicated in all the current slander and calumny, and acquiring gradually the envious and malignant traits of a hackneyed tale-bearer. And the person who, in youth, can attract the attention and win the favor of those of little reflection by flippant and voluble discourse, will encounter in the very same circles neglect, disesteem, and dislike, before the meridian of life is passed; for it takes all the charms that youth, sprightliness, and high animal spirits can furnish, to make an idle tongue fascinating or even endurable.

Let me ask you now to consider for a moment the influence which we exert in conversation upon the happiness or misery of others. It is not too much to say, that most of us do more good or harm in this way than in all other forms beside. Look around you,—take a survey of whatever there is of social or domestic unhappiness in the families to which you belong, or among your kindred and acquaintance. Nine tenths of it can be traced to no other cause than untrue, unkind, or ungoverned speech. A mere harsh word, repented of the next moment,—how great a fire can it kindle! The carrying back and forth of an idle tale, not worth an hour's thought, will often break up the closest intimacies. From every slanderous tongue you may trace numerous rills of bitterness, winding round from house to house, and separating those who ought to be united in the closest friendship. Could persons, who, with kind hearts, are yet hasty in speech, number up, at the close of a day, the feelings that they had wounded, and the uncomfortable sensations that they had caused, they would need no other motive to study suavity of manner, and to seek for their words the rich unction of a truly charitable spirit. Then, too, how many are the traits of suspicion, jealousy, and heart-burning, which go forth from every day's merely idle words, vain and vague surmises, uncharitable inferences and conjectures!

These thoughts point to the necessity of religion as the guiding, controlling element in conversation. All conversation ought to be religious. Not that I would have persons always talking on what are commonly called religious subjects. Let these be talked of at fitting times and places, but never obtrusively brought forward or thrust in. But cannot common subjects be talked of religiously? Cannot we converse about our plans, our amusements, our reading, nay, and our neighbors too, and no sacred name be introduced, and yet the conversation be strictly religious? Yes,—if throughout the conversation we own the laws of honesty, frankness, kind construction, and sincere benevolence,—if our speech be pure, true, gentle, dignified,—if it seek or impart information that either party needs,—if it cherish friendly feeling,—if it give us kinder affections towards others,—if it bring our minds into vigorous exercise,—nay, if it barely amuse us, but not too long, and if the wit be free from coarseness and at no one's expense. But we should ever bear it in mind, that our words are all uttered in the hearing of an unseen Listener and Judge. Could we keep this in remembrance, there would be little in our speech that need give us shame or pain. But that half hour spent in holding up to ridicule one who has done you no harm,—that breathless haste to tell the last piece of slander,—you would not want to remember in your evening prayer. From the flippant, irresponsible, wasteful gossip, in which so much time is daily lost, you could not with a safe conscience look up and own an Almighty presence.

Young ladies, my subject is a large one, and branches out into so many heads, that, were I to say all that I should be glad to say, the setting sun would stop me midway. But it is time for me to relieve your patience. Accept, with these fragmentary hints, my cordial congratulations and good wishes. Life now smiles before you, and beckons you onward. Heaven grant that your coming days may be even happier than you hope! To make them so is within your own power. They will not be cloudless. If you live long, disappointments and sorrows must come. There will be steep and rough passages in the way of life. But there is a Guide, in whose footprints you may climb the steep places without weariness, and tread the rough ground without stumbling. Add to your mental culture faith in Him, and the self-consecration of the Christian heart. Then even trials will make you happier. When clouds are over your way, rays from Heaven will struggle through their fissures, and fringe their edges. Your path will be onward and upward, ever easier, ever brighter. On that path may your early footsteps be planted, that the beautiful bloom of your youth may not wither and perish, but may ripen for a heavenly harvest!

A LECTURE

DELIVERED AT READING, ENGLAND, DECEMBER 19, 1854,
BY FRANCIS TRENCH.

WE are all of us more or less apt to overlook that which is continually going on around us. We omit to make it a matter of inquiry, and reserve our attention for that which is more rare, although of far less importance. What is it, for instance, which, after a course of long, sultry heat,—when the sun, day by day, has blazed in the sky above,—what is it, I ask, which has still preserved the verdure and freshness of all vegetable life? Surely it has been nothing else than the dew of heaven, gently, regularly, plenteously falling, as each evening closed in. Nevertheless, how little is it thought of,—how little are its benefits acknowledged! But when the clouds gather speedily and darkly, and perhaps unexpectedly, when the sense of coolness spreads once more through the parched atmosphere, when abundance of rain all at once descends, then all observe the change, all notice the beneficial results; yet perhaps they are trifling indeed compared with those of the nightly and forgotten dew, which has never ceased to fall, week by week, or even month by month, during the course of the drought. I feel no doubt that it will be acknowledged how it is the same, the very same, in all things calling for our observation. So, therefore, it is regarding conversation, as a thing of every day. We flock to hear and admire some mighty orator's address, but we think little of and little appreciate that daily, hourly thing which is our subject now,—I mean conversation. But I leave you to judge which has the most effect on our general interest, as social creatures,—which, in the long run, has most to do with the pleasure and the profit of all human intercourse.

Having made this claim on your attention, I would now observe that the subject is one of so wide a scope that I can do little more than present you with a few thoughts, which I have noted down as they have risen to my own mind, upon it. And I trust that they will prove not entirely unacceptable, though well indeed aware that the topic is one to which it must be very difficult indeed to do any justice.

But I must first try to meet one objection, for which I am quite prepared, namely, that conversation is not a fit subject for a lecture at all, but should be considered as too independent and free to have any rules, principles, or guidance applied to it. This, however, is indeed a fallacy, and may briefly be exposed by a few such questions as those I am about to ask. What should be more free than the sword of the soldier in the battle-day?—than the pencil of the artist at the mountain side?—or than the poet's song in its upward flight? Yet who would condemn the use of the drill, or the study of perspective, or the rules of poetic art? No less untenable is it to maintain that conversation can be subject to no principle, rule, or review, without checking its free and unfettered range. Cowper has simply summed up the whole truth:—

> "Though conversation in its better part
> May be esteemed a gift, and not an art;
> Yet much depends, as in the tiller's toil,
> On culture and the sowing of the soil."

Nor shall I venture to suggest any measures which I do not believe already well sanctioned, well honored, and well practised too, even by many who have never yet thought of classifying them at all. But these I shall freely give, as my duty is, at your summons this night.

Conversation may be termed or defined as "the exchange and communication, by word, of that which is passing in the inward mind and heart." And none of all known creatures, except man, has this peculiar gift. The animal tribes approach us and even surpass us in many of their physical powers and capacities. As to their capacities in the five senses of the body, I conceive that, generally speaking, it is so; but none of them converse, like man, in expressive words, however they may and do comprehend one another through inferior means. Homer has therefore defined our race as "word-dividing men." And surely such a capacity or power is not bestowed on us unaccompanied by an obligation and a claim to give due diligence how we do and how we may employ it. Never to act thus is surely an undue disregard of our endowment,—a virtual depreciation and contempt of that which is at once among the most needful, the most useful, and, at the same time, most ornamental gifts of God to mankind.

As, then, it is said of real wisdom, that first "it is pure," or free from error and wrong, so too, first of all, right and proper conversation must be free from everything evidently and positively inconsistent with our duty towards God and man. It has ever been well said that we must be just before we are generous. The one attribute is essential and indispensable in every transaction of life. The acts and deeds connected with the other are comparatively undefined and indefinable. So it is essential, it is indispensable, that our conversation, from our own choice and deliberate aim, should be utterly free from all things irreverent to God and injurious to our fellow-creatures. God's name must never be taken in vain. God's Word, and divine things generally, must never be treated with any levity. No sentence must come forth from our lips having any tendency to undermine or subvert the principles and practices of true religion. These are among the mere dues and obligations to Him who gives us the faculty of speech, and enables us to interchange conversation with our fellows; and, beyond all doubt, hour after hour of silence and reserve would be infinitely better—more to be desired by any Christian—than the most entertaining and most captivating talk of a witty but unprincipled man. And so too, exactly, with regard to our fellow-creatures. They too have an absolute claim on us, that we should resolutely keep to the grand rule of speaking to them only such things as will do them no hurt,—no hurt to their minds, no hurt to their feelings, no hurt to their best and true and everlasting interest. As the words of one lead many to heaven and joy, so too the words of another lead many to hell and woe. Better, again I say, would it be for you to be silent as a dumb man than to indulge carelessly and wickedly in any such utterances. He who does it is a cruel enemy of his fellow-creatures, however popular, however able and attractive he may be.

Thus much with regard to conversation—on the negative side. Thus much as to that nature and character of which it must *not* be, under any circumstances. And, having no intention to make my present address in any degree of that more solemn and absolutely serious kind, which it is my privilege so often to employ in my profession, I will only add here that, having now seen what it is essential and indispensable for us to shun in conversation, so again, to aim at pleasing God and serving our fellow-creatures is not less needful,—not less essential, as the one grand object and scope with which at all times we should use and interchange it. I am sure you will all admit that I could not rightly proceed without laying down this broad, this sure foundation. On it we may build the lighter superstructure; but, without laying it down, I could not conscientiously proceed. Nay, farther, I feel equally convinced that many would perceive at once the deficiency, and regret it too, were I to adopt any other course. Conversation, to be worthy of the name at all, is not child's play. It must be dealt with, if considered at all, as an important and substantial thing, not as the mere toy wherewith to trifle and sport each day and hour till we pass away to meet that judgment where our Lord has himself declared,—"By your words ye shall be justified, and by your words ye shall be condemned."

The subject may now branch out into many and various directions. To make a choice is the only difficulty. One of these may lead us to notice that, in all conversation, special attention should ever be paid to the feelings of all present. Every subject should be studiously avoided likely to give needless pain, and perhaps, as it were, open the sluice-gate through which other observations might more plentifully flow in from others of the company, painful to one or more in the circle. Nothing, of course, will teach this so much as true kindness and true sympathy of heart; and, if this be wanting, offences of this kind will continually abound,—yes, I am sorry to say, will sometimes be studiously and intentionally committed. But even the most loving and most kindly spirit will do well to be very watchful on this point, seeking to exercise all judgment and tact in the matter; and even beyond this a beautiful art is sometimes to be witnessed,—happy indeed are they who possess it,—which turns and leads away the general strain of talk, and that often with unperceived skill, when approaching dangerous ground, or perhaps already beginning to grieve or disturb another.

Among injurious practices in talk, the following may perhaps be enumerated:—an overbearing vehemence, challenging assertions, cold indifference to the statements of others, a love of argumentation, an inclination to regard fair liberty of mutual address as undue license, pressure on another to express more than he desires, all personalities which would be forbidden by the royal law of speaking unto others as you would like to be spoken to yourself. These and many more transgressions, in our address one to another, are not only of a grave, but also of a very evident kind, and therefore on them, perhaps, there is less need to dwell.

Others are more subtle,—more elude the grasp of ordinary observation. All social life, and even all family life, if rightly carried on, requires not only mutual forbearance in talk, but mutual sympathy too, mutual encouragement one from the other. In families and in society we find the old, the young; the busy and those comparatively unemployed; the studious or the literary, and those whose tastes are completely different; people occupied in various professions and trades; politicians and statesmen; soldiers and sailors; young men and women reared up at home, with young men and women reared up at schools and public institutions; travellers acquainted with divers parts of the globe, and those who never have quitted their own land; men of the city and men of the field;—in a word, persons and characters almost as various in the aspect of their inward taste as the very features which each countenance wears,—for I may venture to say that no two persons think or feel exactly and altogether alike. Now, whenever there is such a thing as opinion, and whenever there is such a thing as feeling (which is the case in all members of families, and in all members of society with whom you can possibly live or be thrown), there at once is, or there arises, an immediate claim for a kind and proper treatment of these opinions and of these feelings. They may not be your own, they may be utterly different from your own, but that has nothing to do with the question. As a general rule, every one present has no less right to them than you have to yours. You had better go, like Shakspeare's Timon, altogether out of the concourse of your fellow-creatures, if you cannot realize this truth and apply it too. And it is in conversation that you will ever give the chief proofs and evidences whether you do so or not. In it there must be nothing despotic,—nothing to give any present the idea that you have any right to decide what his opinions, what his tastes, what his habits, what his pursuits, should be. You will, of course, not misunderstand me here,—not forget that I am supposing each opinion, each taste, each habit and pursuit, as, on the face of it, allowable and innocent, although not yours. I repeat it, there must be no despotism in society. Equality must prevail as a general rule; I say a general rule, because there are, no doubt, certain seasons and times when the intercourse of social and of family life must partake of that special character which is adapted to the various relationships of man. The parent must, at times, simply direct the child by his words. The teacher, authoritatively, must instruct the pupil. The master or employer must tell the employed what to do. And occasionally, in society, the rule above laid down will, by general consent, lie in abeyance, if it may be so expressed. And, on certain subjects,—I mean those whereon we are ourselves ignorant, but others in our company are highly informed,—we may be content to be just listeners, merely demonstrating that sympathy and interest adequate to keep up the flow of instruction from another's lips. But intercourse of this kind scarcely can be termed conversation; and when circumstances like these occur in social and family life, they must be directed by other rules not altogether applicable to our present subject. Now, to enter with full sympathy into the claims of all present in society for this equal right of interchanged sentiment, and to show this feeling at times by patient forbearance and at other times by manifest appreciation of that which others say, is no slight grace and gift. And here the various lessons on the subject, which experience or observation has taught, must be brought into play; and the information in any way gained as to the various feelings, habits, and tastes ordinarily entertained by people of different ages, different professions, and different characters, must be judiciously applied. Nor will this, in the least, spoil free and fair discussion of any topic. On the contrary, it will promote it. And thus that principle will be rightly maintained which I have endeavored to lay down and commend, viz., that when any special opinion, feeling, or taste is expressed in society,—I mean, of course, in a proper and legitimate way,—it should always be treated by all present with that measure of respect which each one would wish exercised towards himself for his own personal views. Just in proportion as men are boorish, coarse, and unsocial, in the true and extensive sense of the word, will they transgress here. Yes, even put together one, ungainly tempered, from his field, and another of the same character from his shop or counting house, and very likely not five minutes will elapse before one or the other will say something to disparage those habits and tastes with which he himself happens to be not conversant. There ensues discord and disseverance, or, it may be, silence and separation. But, on the other hand, just in proportion as you are enabled to unite yourself with others through your demeanor and words,—not, of course, hypocritically or obsequiously, but from real sympathy with all the innocent tastes and engagements of our fellow-creatures,—just, I say, in proportion as you are enabled to do this, will your intercourse with them, in the way of conversation, be of that kind at which we should aim. None will be afraid of your indulging in rebuffs, or ridicule, or depreciation. None will meet from you a cold, heartless, and repulsive indifference. To you, and before you, the flower[A] of each human heart (if I may so speak) will then have a tendency to open and expand its varied forms and hues, instead of retaining them all closed and shut up; and many, many thoughts will be expressed to you and before you which will never be heard, or at all events rarely, indeed, by those of a sneering, unsympathizing, hard, and ungenial spirit. Thus you will be known, or rather felt, instinctively felt, as one who will do nothing to chill, but, on the contrary, much to encourage that free spirit (in the best sense of the word) which should mark and imbue all social intercourse deserving the name at all; and you will be welcomed by all who can appreciate good taste, good tact, and (I will add) good feeling too,—for that is the chief spring of all such conduct; and you will be enabled to receive and communicate much pleasure and profit too, wheresoever you may go.

A word here may not be inappropriate as to what is sometimes called "drawing a person out"—*i. e.* leading another to tell you, or any company assembled in your presence, what they know, what they have seen, what they feel, what, in a word, they are able to communicate, if so disposed and led. Now, this drawing out is a very delicate affair. When successfully done, it is most valuable. When the attempt proves unsuccessful, you are very likely to lose or interfere with the very object in view. Questioning of all kinds,—up from that on the simplest topic, and with a purpose of the simplest kind, to that involving the most important results,—questioning, I say, of all kinds, requires judgment and tact. Many persons much err in this department of address. Some err by asking about matters on which it is quite clear that they have no real feeling and concern. Some err by demands as to your own personal proceedings, wherewith they have no connection. Some, again, err by putting questions, not wrongly or inappropriately, but merely too many at a time, or in too rapid a succession. This scarcely can be called conversation at all,—and, generally speaking, (though I do not deny that there are exceptions, which will at once recur to the intelligent,) yes, generally speaking, is most unsatisfactory. And the reason, if we analyze the matter, is, that all the statements, or observations, or call them what you will, proceed, under such circumstances, from one of the parties engaged. It is not reciprocal; it is not mutually communicated with due equality of interchanged thought. You will at once perceive that this must be detrimental; and I would suggest that when you may observe the damage which is thus done to conversation, you should seek at once to put the discourse on a better plan,—to shift it, as it were, on a better line for good progress. And that may sometimes be done by putting a question to those who question you, or even more, by making the number of questions on each side, in some measure, to correspond. This, of course, must not be done harshly or abruptly, nor so as to give the very least impression that you yourself desire to withhold and draw in; but it may often be advantageously done; and you will thus afford to another the natural and fit means of telling you something, as a response for that which you tell him. Then true conversation will begin; then the due interchange of expression, which alone merits the name; then each party becomes rightly placed, and the intercourse will improve almost instantaneously.

But if, in these very commonest forms of our mutual address, it is not an easy thing to put questions well,—neither too many, nor in their wrong place,—then we may be well assured that it is more difficult still when the object, expressly, is to lead on another, gifted perhaps in many ways, or having perhaps some special thing to tell, unknown to you or others present. And yet what a valuable art this is! Much is lost in society by incapacity for its due exercise. Much is gained by skill in its employment. But many reasons concur to render it very difficult. The following may be mentioned among many others. Some are full of matter, but shy or reserved. Some are unaware of the deep interest which certain things, well known to them, would have for others, if they would communicate them; (in illustration of this, I may perhaps quote scientific men, travellers, those who have led strange and peculiar lives.) Some are too modest to put themselves in any prominent light. Others are too proud so to do, lest they should fail in winning full attention to their words. Some are jaded and worn with previous hours of intellectual toil, and the current of their thoughts is still flowing on in a channel of its own. Some are laboring under a kind of awe of one or more persons in the company. Some are young, and scarcely seem to realize or know how acceptable are the thoughts and fresh expressions of youth to those of maturer years. Others are afraid of being too professional in their remarks. Others are indolent in the use of their tongue and utterance. And numerous other causes might be mentioned, which sadly interfere with the full, free, and general flow of discourse or conversation. And yet, at the same time, there may be rich stores in the assembly,—much, very much, to communicate,—something, at least, in each either to please, or inform and improve,—something perhaps in every one present which, if told and expressed to those around him, would add and contribute no slight nor unprized contribution to the common stock. But how to elicit it—there is the difficulty. Nevertheless, very much may be done by tact and kindness, by animation and by cordiality, by watching and waiting for fit opportunities, by that appreciation of each one in the circle which will encompass and arouse all, as it were, with a kind of electric chain,—by a constant and deliberate aim to converse yourself at the time when it may be requisite, and willingly to lapse into silence and the background when another takes up the subject. And, although it is a measure which requires no little taste and moderation in its use, still it is sometimes not only very graceful, but very effectual too, if you will open out on some few personal topics which may concern yourself, and thus win a response from others present, who may personally know or have personally gone through that which you and others in the company would desire, and rightly desire, to hear opened out without any reserve.

In order, again, to promote conversation of a superior sort, endeavor must be made to expand and enlarge its bounds to the very utmost. It should be of a comprehensive kind,—not the gossip of some narrow set, not a mere comment on the persons and affairs of any one locality, not a wearisome and dull repetition of things already, perhaps long, familiar to all present. I repeat, it should be comprehensive,—brought forward, as it were, from a full treasury of "things new and old," and coined into various sums, larger for such occasions as may need, and small—yes, even to the smallest—for the fit use and time. It should be formed of various materials, of that which has been seen, and heard, and read. A monotonous character is fatal to it. At one time it should arouse and awaken,—at another it should calm and soothe. At one time it should lead into deep and grave questions,—at another it should play lightly over the surface of things. At one time it may touch the spirit of the hearer, almost into tears,—at another it may raise the full freedom of laughter and mirth. At one time it may be addressed to all within the convenient reach of your words,—at another to one listening ear. If possible, it should touch on many tastes, on many places, on various interests, giving to each present (however different each taste and character) the best and fairest opening for a share in the circling talk, which opportunity every one, at fit occasion and turn, should be willing to embrace, and thus to render his or her social dues to those who freely and fairly contribute theirs. No one, on the other hand, should seek dominion, nor ever two or three, over the remainder. Again, conversation should never be allowed so to fall into separate or little knots, that one here or one there should remain alone or excluded altogether. It should be carried on in appropriate tones of voice. They should be somewhat raised, or rather, I would say, strengthened for the old and for those who are a little deaf, of whom there are many. This, however, not too obviously; not to remind any of infirmity. They should be quick, firm, and spirited for those in middle age, with their faculties in full strength. They should be somewhat gentler to the young, lest they be at all checked; and somewhat slower, that they may have more time and means to frame their own answer. For which the reason is, that as "practice makes perfect" in all things, so they, whose practice has, of course, been less than their seniors', need more time to make up for the want of it, even in conversation. At all times discourse is liable to alternations as to its interest and life. Expect this, and even should it become at any moment what is called dull, or even should an awkward pause and silence come on, do not seem to notice it. This will only make it worse. Rather try yourself to gather up the broken thread, or to introduce some new matter. Every one should avoid bringing forward or needlessly dwelling on any topic whatsoever likely to affect any others present with any unfavorable reminiscences. The wealthy will avoid, as a general rule, allusions to their property and wealth before any persons who, although their equals in society, are known to be of poor and inadequate estate. The healthy and the vigorous of frame will not forget that others are invalids; those free as air in the disposition of their time, that others have but very little, and that with difficulty spared; the quick and intelligent, that others are more slow in apprehension; those of hardy spirit, well strung and braced, that others are nervous, sensitive, and tried by words, tones, gestures, and expressions, which would not try, nor vex, or affect them in the least degree. But what tact is requisite in all this! And many, many failures must there be; sins of commission and of omission too, even among those who earnestly seek in this matter to fulfil, always and everywhere, the rules of true courtesy, and, which is better still, the rules of true Christian love. Nevertheless, the aim at which we point is by no means without its value as a profitable exercise both of the mind and heart. No, nor is it ineffectual and unblessed. For, although at times words may be said which we would long to recall, and strings of feeling touched by our utterance which afterthought tells us we should not have moved, and topics handled with much want of that skill and judgment which we should have wished most truly to employ, still, with a good aim before us, and with right principles in some measure realized, and seeking to correct any error when discovered, as well as to advance more in all which improves and adorns right social intercourse, much will be done towards the goodly end. And large indeed will be the amount of pleasure and of benefit which you may thus hope to reap for yourself and communicate to others in the course of your life, and that, too, up to an age, should your days be prolonged, when you may be shut up, or at all events much restrained, from many other means of active usefulness. For the mellowed wisdom of age, showing and expressing itself in that charity and sympathy for all which nothing less than experience itself has taught, is indeed a strong and beautiful thing.

Hitherto I have spoken altogether on conversation with those whose rank and position of life corresponds with your own. A few words now on conversation, first, with those of a higher rank, and, secondly, with those in the humbler conditions of life—to use the common phrase; and every man should be qualified and prepared for any and for all kinds of association.

To those of a higher rank than ourselves we may, without derogating in the least from our independence and self-respect, show that deference which not only the customs of all nations, but the Scripture also most evidently inculcates. This, of course, will appear when engaged with them in conversation. It will, however, be shown rather in some occasional acknowledgment than in the manner or matter of discourse. The rank of another does not in the least demand that you should surrender your opinion to his, nor conceal your sentiments, nor assume any other line of subjects and topics than you would address to those more immediately your equals in worldly position. A vague, undefined notion seems to float through each rank of society in our land, that those in the stage above think, feel, and act in a manner different from those below. A very great mistake this, which oftentimes chills and checks and mars all open freedom of address when one of an higher and one of a lower rank are brought into those circumstances where the opportunity for conversation occurs, if not the absolute claim. But let it be remembered that the mind and heart of man or of woman varies but little through these mere distinctions of the world. I do not say that it does not vary at all, but very little. The main current of joy, the main current of sorrow, is the same in all classes, though the lesser streams may variously and separately flow. The main current of affections, of interests, is the same. All are subject to the same need of kind, friendly sympathy; all are made to interchange thought; all share in the manifold impressions of our common nature. Wealth and nobility, and rank and station, are, after all, only artificial things, not the main staple of life in any man or woman. When, therefore, you are brought into the society of one or more like these, be to them appropriately courteous. Acknowledge their position at once, and then let your intercourse with them flow freely on, just as with others. Trouble not them, nor trouble yourself, with any other system of address. Deprive not them, nor deprive yourself, of free, open, natural communication. And, depend upon it, that acting and speaking thus, you will not only be oftentimes pleased rather than silenced and embarrassed by such society, but you will be sure to please and to be valued,—yes, and to meet no less friendly sympathy, both of mind and heart, than is to be found in each other rank of life.

And now a few words on conversation with our poorer friends or neighbors, or any persons in this class of life with whom, habitually, we may have to do, or whom we may meet at any time or place. And few of that class being, I conclude, here, I may speak to you as those who would gladly receive any hints for kind consideration as to the right way of fulfilling your own part in this matter. For I, too, would wish to be a learner on it, so important do I conceive it to be. So much has been said, and so much has been written, on the benefit of free, kindly intercourse between the rich and the poor, the employers and the employed, those who labor with their heads and those who labor with their hands, that any mere general or vague observations on the subject would be quite out of place here. I shall, accordingly, regard you not only as admitting this truth, but also as desirous yourselves to exemplify it; and, again, as admitting, and feeling too, that merely to pay wages, and to give directions and commands, and to bestow alms, and to support charitable institutions (however needful and good such things may be), is not enough for one desiring to secure the sympathy and love of his poorer brethren. For that you must be ready, willing, able to converse with them. To qualify yourself for doing this, is in many professions an indispensable and most evident duty,—for instance, with the ministers of religion and with medical men. They could do nothing without such conversation. And, considering it due at proper seasons from every one in a higher class of life to those below them, I shall just offer you a few hints, which seem to me not unworthy of note. Avoid, then, on the one hand, all hard, overbearing address; while, on the other, there must be energy, spirit, firmness, and life. Avoid all semblance of patronage and condescension, but at the same time never make any forced attempts to appear what you are not, or to assume a character not your own. Do not imagine the range of subjects small; and, when you can, choose those topics in which you and those addressed both take an interest. Many there are common to all classes. Be not impatient to come to a point too quick, but give people a full opportunity to express themselves in their own way; nor count this waste time. It is very much otherwise. Use short rather than long sentences,—language colloquial, not that of books,—giving emphasis, tone, and strength to your words,—never lapsing into cold, lifeless, inexpressive tones. Trust oftentimes, in conversation with the poor and comparatively uneducated, that there is much more intelligence within than the answer which they make in words would lead you, at first sight, to expect. Be willing and ready to tell something about yourself, your family, and concerns, when there appears any interest about them. Remember that family ties and affections are strong in one as in another of the human family; and, as among your own friends and associates you would refer to these natural topics, so do here. Let wants and necessities, and trials and difficulties, not be forgotten, but let them not be the whole subject-matter of discourse. No, let it range far more widely, far more attractively; and your looks and your demeanor, and your tones and words, being all directed by good will, and by practice too, you indeed will be no idler in good works during times and occasions thus employed. You will win much love, much esteem, much appreciation; you will hear much right feeling expressed, and, at times, much to inform you of a practical kind. You will do good and receive good too.

It appears to me that I have now presented to your notice almost a sufficiency of topics, relative to conversation, for one single lecture. Nevertheless, I feel unwilling to conclude without drawing your attention to a few facts connected with the subject. One is, that the ablest and mightiest authors of all times and countries have borne their strong testimony to the attraction which conversation presents, by casting a large portion of their writings into this form or mould. Thus did Homer in poetry, Plato in philosophy, and dramatists, of all ages, in their plays. Thus did Cicero in his various treatises; and Horace appears[B] talking to you in many and many a page. Dante's grand poem, "Il Purgatorio," is chiefly a conversation. The French have ever excelled in such writings; and of such a character is that well-known gem in the literature of Spain, I of course allude to "Don Quixote." In Shakspeare and Walter Scott it is the same, and they, perhaps, are the most popular writers of our land, except one. Who, do you ask, is that? John Bunyan, the author of the "Pilgrim's Progress;" but that very book comes up with its testimony too, being a dialogue throughout,—rich in pathos and wit, rich in illustration, rich in experience, rich in all variety and combination,—in a word, the very perfection of talk; not less attractive than it is weighty, not less entertaining than heavenly, holy, and full of all things which make a book precious.

But another book there is, of which it is well said:—

> "A glory gilds the sacred page,
> Majestic like the sun!
> It gives a light to every age;
> It gives, but borrows none."

And in that book of books there are four short but most mighty narratives. And each of those narratives contains the one most important record which ever had to be told upon this earth. Each of them gives one concurrent history; namely, that of the life of our Lord Jesus Christ, with his sayings and his deeds. And of conversation these holy narratives are full. God has chosen this mode of reaching our minds and influencing our hearts, by large —very large—portions of them written after this fashion. Cowper felt this so deeply, that, in his poem on our present subject, he has beautifully told and paraphrased all that went on when Jesus met and talked with the two disciples on the way to Emmaus. Moreover, in those gospels, there is one, penned by that "disciple whom Jesus loved;" and if there is much conversation in all four of them, in it especially—in the gospel of St. John —conversation appears in all its full and continued glory. Take one or two examples. Mankind, all mankind, had to be taught about the complete atonement for our sins made by our Saviour on the cross. Where is it more clearly, more mightily told than in the third chapter of St. John's gospel? But what is that chapter? Is it a law prescribed in set terms?—No. Is it a sermon?—No. Is it a mere address?—No. You will all remember it is a conversation,—Christ's conversation with Nicodemus by night. And so it is again in the very next chapter, where a subject of no less importance—I say it advisedly, no less importance—is set forth, viz. the work of the Holy Spirit in man's heart; and that is portrayed for us in a conversation with the woman of Samaria, at Sychar's well. What striking instances are these! And many others might be added to them. And thus we have before us even the sanction and proof from the Word of God, that the most mighty and transcendent truth can reach us in no better form than that which conversation gives, and also that Jesus Christ put his own royal stamp of glory on it, by employing it Himself continually, when upon the earth among men, though he was their Lord and their God.

Having thus been led on,—I think very naturally, and, as I think, quite appropriately, too, for one of my office and position, at any time or place, or on any subject,—I will not return to any lighter theme. I do not in the least regret that I have selected my present topic out of very many which suggested themselves to my mind, when I was asked to exercise the privilege of thus addressing you, as I have now done for these four years. I might have chosen others far more entertaining, and, no doubt, some far more kindling and exciting at this present time,[C] when our thoughts and our feelings are all so concentrated on one distant spot of strife and of contest, and of danger, and of bravery, and wounds, and deaths, and bereavements,—and amidst all, of honor unexampled to our brave brethren in arms. But, for many reasons, I have done otherwise. I have chosen, as usual, a subject of general, of national, of wide-world, of never-failing interest, from day to day, from week to week, from month to month, from year to year, among the vast race of our fellows,—born social creatures, born for mutual sympathy, with interchanged utterance, speech, and conversation. Strongly do I feel its importance, and I cannot help expressing my surprise that so little, so very little, has systematically been written or said upon it. I have found it no ordinary theme, I assure you; and, though it is one on which we all instinctively are interested in any circle, or with whomsoever we may at any time be, still it is not one on which the arrangement and classification of thought is an easy thing. I therefore shall not feel disappointed, nor, do I trust, will you be disappointed either, in that good employment of your time which you have a right to expect from me, as your lecturer to-night here, if I shall have set before you any thoughts, for your attention, which may improve, in the least degree, the course and the current of ordinary conversation. When we remember how much of our innocent gratification,—how much of our daily harmony one with another, —how much of our mutual improvement,—depends on the right exercise of this goodly gift,—then, I am sure, you will not consider that the subject is one to be neglected or ignored. I verily believe that I do not over-state the fact, in asserting that for one time when we are liable to hurt, or distress, or offend another by our acts and deeds, there are fifty or an hundred, or perhaps more, occasions, when we are liable to do so by our words, and demeanor, and utterance. And again, for once that we can do kind and profitable actions to those around us, and associating with us, there are fifty or an hundred,—perhaps more occasions still,—when we can please or profit another by our words. I ask you, as those who can judge in this matter for yourselves, "Is it not so? Is it not so most undeniably?" Well, then, if I have been successful in laying down any right principles, in exposing anything disadvantageous, or in presenting any available means for rendering your daily intercourse more evidently kind, more evidently sympathizing, more evidently, in a word, such as that which every good man would wish to exhibit, and which must render him not only welcome and not only useful, but a real and true ornament of society in the best sense of the word; if I have shown you anything whatever available to this end, whether for your use at home or abroad, in the cottage or the shop, in the humblest abode or in the noblest and in the wealthiest, then surely I shall not have spoken in vain. I speak on no narrow topic, and I speak for all. Truly it is one which touches all; and in this lies its strength and its interest. There is no one, I believe, who does not intuitively and instinctively feel either his gain or his loss in conversation,—the effect of it on his own mind and on his own feelings at the time and afterwards,—either its harms or its charms. All must feel this, though unable perhaps to classify their thoughts or express them on it, and perhaps they have never thought of so doing. And I, for one, will not hesitate to say that, it having been my lot to mix much, and willingly, in all the various classes of society,—and having endeavored, so far as in my power has been, to cultivate and show a true brotherly and friendly spirit, both to high and low,—I have met nothing to confer more pleasure and more advantage in daily life than fit conversation. I have found it from the poorest. I have found it from those of middle station. I have found it among the noble and the rich. And, while without it the hours of social and of family life may drag on heavily, and in a wearisome and worthless way, under the roofs of splendor and magnificence, and in the midst of feasts, and pomp, and parade, with it, freely interchanged from well-informed heads and cordial hearts, expressing what they know and telling what they feel, without any restraint except that of love, and tact, and propriety,—with it, I say, the simplest home may be one of enjoyment and improvement every recurring day, and each coming guest will share its attractions,—and therefore I say to every one present, "Despise not this gift, and try to improve it; and seek Divine help for its right regulation, as well as for its use; and be well assured that, under God's blessing, in its direction you will gain for yourself, and promote for your fellow-creatures, no slight share of true enjoyment, no slight benefits both for this world and for the world to come."

INTRODUCTION.

It is readily acknowledged, by all well educated foreigners, that English Grammar is very easy to learn, the difficulties of the language lying in the numberless variations and licenses of its pronunciation. Since to us then, children of the soil, pronunciation has no difficulties to offer, is it not a reproach that so many speak their own language in an inelegant and slatternly manner,—either through an inexcusable ignorance of grammatical rules, or a wanton violation of them? There are two sorts of bad speakers,— the educated and the uneducated. I write for the former, and I shall deal the less leniently with them, because "where much is given, much will be expected." Ay, and where much has been achieved too, and intellectual laurels have been gathered, is it not a reproach that a *slatternly* mode of expression should sometimes deteriorate from the eloquence of the scholar, and place the accomplished man or woman, in *this* respect, on a level with the half-educated or the illiterate?

Some one, I think it is Lord Chesterfield, has wisely said, "Whatever is worth doing, is worth doing well." Then, if our native language is worth studying, surely it is worth *speaking well*, and as there is no standing still in excellence of any kind, so, even in language,—in so simple a thing as the expression of our thoughts by words,—if we do not improve we shall retrograde.

It is a common opinion that a knowledge of Latin supersedes the necessity of the study of English grammar. This must entail a strong imputation of carelessness on our Latin students, who sometimes commit such solecisms in English as make us regret they did not *once*, at least, peruse the grammatical rules of their native language.

We laugh at the blunders of a foreigner, but perpetrate our own offences with so much gravity that an observer would have a right to suppose we consider them what they really are,—*no laughing matter*.

CHAPTER I.

I.

Some people speak of "so many *spoonsfull*," instead of "so many spoonfuls." The rule on this subject says: "Compounds ending in *ful*, and all those in which the principal word is put last, form the plural in the same manner as other nouns,—as 'handfuls, spoonfuls, mouthfuls,'" &c., &c.

Logic will demonstrate the propriety of this rule. Are you measuring by a plurality of spoons? If so, "so many *spoonsfull*" must be the correct term; but if the process of measuring be effected by *refilling the same spoon*, then it becomes evident that the precise idea meant to be conveyed is, the *quantity* contained in the vessel by which it is measured, which is a "*spoonful*."

II.

It is a common mistake to speak of "a disagreeable effluvia." This word is *effluvium* in the singular, and *effluvia* in the plural. The same rule should be observed with *automaton, arcanum, erratum, phenomenon, memorandum*, and several others which are less frequently used, and which change the *um* or *on* into *a*, to form the plural. It is so common a thing, however, to say *memorandums*, that I fear it would sound a little pedantic, in colloquial style, to use the word *memoranda*; and it is desirable, perhaps, that custom should make an exception of this word, as well as of *encomium*, and allow two terminations to it, according to the taste of the speaker and the style of the discourse,—*memorandums* or *memoranda*, like *encomiums* or *encomia*.

III.

We have heard *pulse* and *patience* treated as pluralities, much to our astonishment.

IV.

It seems to be a position assumed by all grammarians, that their readers already understand the meaning of the word "case," as applied to nouns and pronouns; hence they never enter into a clear explanation of the simple term, but proceed at once to a discussion of its grammatical distinctions, in which it frequently happens that the student, for want of a little introductory explanation, is unable to accompany them. But I am not going to repeat to the scholar how the term "case" is derived from a Latin word signifying "to fall," and is so named because all the other cases *fall* or *decline* from the nominative, in order to express the various relations of nouns to each other,—which in Latin they do by a difference of termination, in English by the aid of prepositions,—and that an orderly arrangement of all these different terminations is called the declension of a noun, &c. I am not going to repeat to the scholar the things he already knows; but to you, my gentle readers, to whom Latin is still an unknown tongue, to whom grammars are become obsolete things, and grammatical definitions would be bewildering preliminaries, "more honored in the breach than in the observance,"—to you I am anxious to explain, in the clearest manner practicable, all the mysteries of this case, because it was a cruel perplexity to myself in days of yore. And I will endeavor to make my lecture as brief and clear as possible, requesting you to bear in mind that no knowledge is to be acquired without a little trouble; and that whosoever may consider it too irksome a task to exert the understanding for a *short* period, must be content to remain in inexcusable and irremediable ignorance. Though, I doubt not, when you come to perceive how great the errors are which you daily commit, you will not regret having sat down quietly for half an hour to listen to an unscholastic exposition of them.

V.

We all understand the meaning of the word "case," as it is applied to the common affairs of life; but when we meet with it in our grammars, we view it as an abstruse term. We will not consent to believe that it means nothing more than *position of affairs*, *condition*, or *circumstances*, any one of which words might be substituted for it with equal propriety, if it were not indispensable in grammar to adhere strictly to the same term when we wish to direct the attention unerringly to the same thing, and to keep the understanding alive to the justness of its application; whilst a multiplicity of names to one thing would be likely to create confusion. Thus, if one were to say, "This is a very hard case," or "A singular case occurred the other day," or "That poor man's case is a very deplorable one," we should readily comprehend that by the word "case" was meant "circumstance" or "situation;" and when we speak, in the language of the grammar, of "a noun in the nominative case," we only mean a person or thing placed in such circumstances as to become merely named, or named as the performer of some action,—as "the man," or "the man walks." In both these sentences, "man" is in the nominative case; because in the first he is simply *named*, without reference to any circumstance respecting him, and in the second he is named as the performer of the *act* of *walking* mentioned. When we speak of a noun in the possessive case, we simply mean a person or thing placed under such circumstances as to become named as the *possessor* of something; and when we speak of a noun in the objective case, we only intend to express a person or thing standing in such a situation as to be, in some way or other, affected by the act of some other person or thing,—as "Henry teaches Charles." Here Henry is, by an abbreviation of terms, called *the nominative case*, (instead of the *noun* in the nominative case,) because he stands in that situation in which it is incumbent on us to name him as the *performer* of the act of teaching; and Charles is, by the same abbreviating license, called the *objective case*, because he is in such a position of affairs as to *receive* the act of teaching which Henry performs. I will now tell you how you may always distinguish the three cases. Read the sentence attentively, and understand accurately what the nouns are represented as doing. If any person or thing be represented as *performing* an *action*, that person or thing is a noun in the nominative case. If any person or thing be represented as *possessing something*, that person or thing is a noun in the possessive case. And if any person or thing be represented as neither performing nor possessing, it is a noun in the objective case, whether directly or indirectly affected by the action of the nominative; because, as we have in English but *three* cases, which contain the substance of the *six Latin* cases, *whatever is neither nominative nor possessive must be objective*. Here I might wander into a long digression on passive and neuter verbs, which I may seem to have totally overlooked in the principle just laid down; but I am not writing a grammar,—not attempting to illustrate the various ramifications of grammatical laws to people who know nothing at all about them,—any more than I am writing for the edification of the accomplished scholar, to whom purity of diction is already familiar. I am writing, chiefly, for that vast portion of the educated classes who have never looked into a grammar since their school days were over, but who have ingeniously hewn out for themselves a middle path between ignorance and knowledge, and to whom certain little hillocks in their way have risen up, under a dense atmosphere, to the magnitude of mountains. I merely wish to give to them, since they will not take the trouble to search for themselves, one broad and general principle, unclogged by exceptions, to guide them to propriety of speech; and should they afterwards acquire a taste for grammatical disputation, they will of course apply to more extensive sources for the necessary qualifications.

VI.

It is scarcely possible to commit any inaccuracy in the use of these cases when restricted to nouns, but in the application of them to pronouns a woful confusion often arises; though even in this confusion exists a marked distinction between the errors of the ill-bred and those of the well-bred man. To use the objective instead of the nominative is a *vulgar* error; to use the nominative instead of the objective is a *genteel* error. No person of decent education would think of saying, "Him and me are going to the play." Yet how often do we hear even well educated people say, "They were coming to see my brother and *I*,"—"The claret will be packed in two hampers for Mr. Smith and *I*,"—"Let you and *I* try to move it,"—"Let him and *I* go up and speak to them,"—"Between you and *I*," &c. &c.;—faults as heinous as that of the vulgarian who says, "Him and me are going to the play," and with less excuse. Two minutes' reflection will enable the scholar to correct himself, and a little exercise of memory will shield him from a repetition of the fault; but, for the benefit of those who may *not* be scholars, we will accompany him through the mazes of his reflections. Who are the persons that are performing the act of "coming to see"? "*They*." Then the pronoun *they* must stand in the nominative case. Who are the persons to whom the act of "coming to see" extends? "My brother and I." Then "my brother and I," being the *objects affected* by the act of the nominative, must be a noun and pronoun standing in the objective case; and as nouns are not susceptible of change on account of cases, it is only the *pronoun* which requires alteration to render the sentence correct: "They were coming to see my brother and *me*." The same argument is applicable to the other examples given. In the English language, the imperative mood of a verb is never conjugated with a pronoun in the nominative case, therefore, "Let you and *I* try to move it," "Let him and *I* go up and speak to them," are manifest improprieties. A very simple test may be formed by taking away the first noun or pronoun from the sentence altogether, and bringing the verb or preposition right against that pronoun which you use to designate yourself: thus, "They were coming to see *I*," "The claret will be packed in two hampers for *I*," "Let *I* try to move it," &c. By this means your own ear will correct you, without any reference to grammatical rules. And bear in mind that the number of *nouns* it may be necessary to press into the sentence will not alter the *case* respecting the pronouns.

"Between you and I" is as erroneous an expression as any. Change the position of the pronouns, and say, "Between I and you;" or change the sentence altogether, and say, "Between I and the wall there was a great gap;" and you will soon see in what case the first person should be rendered. "Prepositions govern the objective case," therefore it is impossible to put a nominative *after* a preposition without a gross violation of a rule which ought to be familiar to everybody.

VII.

The same mistake extends to the relative pronouns "who" and "whom." We seldom hear the objective case used either by vulgar or refined speakers. "Who did you give it to?" "Who is this for?" are solecisms of daily occurrence; and when the objective "whom" *is* used, it is generally put in the wrong place; as, "The person whom I expected would purchase that estate," "The man whom they intend shall execute that work." This intervening verb in each sentence, "I expected" and "they intend," coming between the last verb and its own nominative (the relative pronoun), has no power to alter the rule, and no right to violate it; but as the introduction of an intervening verb, in such situations, is likely to beguile the ear and confuse the judgment, it would be better to avoid such constructions altogether, and turn the sentence in a different way; as, "The person whom I expected *to be* the purchaser of that estate," "The man whom they intend *to* execute that work." If the reader will cut off the intervening verb, which has nothing to do with the construction of the sentence, except to mystify it, he will perceive at a glance the error and its remedy: "The person *whom* would purchase that estate," "The man *whom* shall execute that work."

VIII.

It is very easy to mistake the nominative when another noun comes between it and the verb, which is frequently the case in the use of the indefinite and distributive pronouns; as, "One of those houses *were* sold last week," "Each of the daughters *are* to have a separate share," "Every tree in those plantations *have* been injured by the storm," "Either of the children *are* at liberty to claim it." Here it will be perceived that the pronouns "one," "each," "every," "either," are the true nominatives to the verbs; but the intervening noun in the plural number, in each sentence, deludes the ear, and the speaker, without reflection, renders the verb in the plural instead of the singular number. The same error is often committed when no second noun appears to plead an apology for the fault; as, "Each city *have their* peculiar privileges," "Everybody has a right to look after *their* own interest," "Either *are* at liberty to claim it." This is the effect of pure carelessness.

IX.

There is another very common error, the reverse of the last mentioned, which is that of rendering the adjective pronoun in the *plural* number instead of the singular in such sentences as the following: "*These* kind of entertainments are not conducive to general improvement," "*Those* sort of experiments are often dangerous." This error seems to originate in the habit which people insensibly acquire of supposing the prominent noun in the sentence (such as "entertainments" or "experiments") to be the noun qualified by the adjective "these" or "those;" instead of which it is "kind," "sort," or any word of that description *immediately following* the adjective, which should be so qualified, and the adjective must be made to agree with it in the singular number. We confess it is not so agreeable to the ear to say, "*This* kind of entertainments," "*That* sort of experiments;" but it would be easy to give the sentence a different form, and say, "Entertainments of this kind," "Experiments of that sort," by which the requisitions of grammar would be satisfied, and those of euphony too.

X.

But the grand fault, the glaring impropriety, committed by "all ranks and conditions of men," rich and poor, high and low, illiterate and learned,—except, perhaps, one in twenty,—and from which not even the pulpit or the bar is totally free,—is, the substitution of the active verb *lay* for the neuter verb *lie* (to lie down). The scholar *knows* that "active verbs govern the objective case," and therefore *demand* an objective case after them; and that neuter verbs *will not admit* an objective case after them, *except* through the medium of a preposition. *He*, therefore, has no excuse for his error, it is a wilful one; for him the following is not written. And here I may as well say, once for all, that whilst I would *remind* the *scholar* of his lapses, my instructions and explanations are offered *only* to the class which requires them.

"To lay" is an active transitive verb, like *love, demanding* an objective case after it, *without the intervention of a preposition*. "To lie" is a neuter verb, *not admitting an objective case after it, except through the intervention of a preposition;*—yet this "perverse generation" *will* go on substituting the former for the latter. Nothing can be more erroneous than to say, as people constantly do, "I shall go and lay down." The question which naturally arises in the mind of the discriminating hearer is, "*What* are you going to lay down,—money, carpets, plans, or what?" for, as a transitive verb is used, an object is wanted to complete the sense. The speaker means, in fact, to tell us that he (himself) is going to *lie down*, instead of which he gives us to understand that he is going to *lay* down or *put* down something which he has not named, but which it is necessary to name before we can understand the sentence; and this sentence, when completed according to the rules of grammar, will never convey the meaning he intends. One might as well use the verb "to put" in this situation, as the verb "to lay," for each is a transitive verb, requiring an objective case immediately after it. If you were to enter a room, and, finding a person lying on the sofa, were to address him with such a question as "What are you doing there?" you would think it ludicrous if he were to reply, "I am *putting* down;" yet it would not be more absurd than to say, "I am *laying* down;" but custom, whilst it fails to reconcile us to the error, has so familiarized us with it, that we hear it without surprise, and good breeding forbids our noticing it to the speaker. The same mistake is committed through all the tenses of the verb. How often are nice ears wounded by the following expressions,—"My brother *lays* ill of a fever,"—"The vessel *lays* in St. Katharine's Docks,"—"The books were *laying* on the floor,"—"He *laid* on a sofa three weeks,"—"After I had *laid* down, I remembered that I had left my pistols *laying* on the table." You must perceive that, in every one of these instances, the wrong verb is used; correct it, therefore, according to the explanation given; thus, "My brother *lies* ill of a fever,"—"The vessel *lies* in St Katherine's Docks,"—"The books were *lying* on the floor,"—"He *lay* on a sofa three weeks,"—"After I had *lain* down, I remembered that I had left my pistols *lying* on the table."

It is probable that this error has originated in the circumstance of the present tense of the verb "to lay" being conjugated precisely like the imperfect tense of the verb "to lie," for they are alike in orthography and sound, and different only in meaning; and in order to remedy the evil which this resemblance seems to have created, I have conjugated at full length the simple tenses of the two verbs, hoping the exposition may be found useful; for it is an error which *must* be corrected by all who aspire to the merit of speaking their own language *well*.

Verb Active.
To lay.
Present tense.

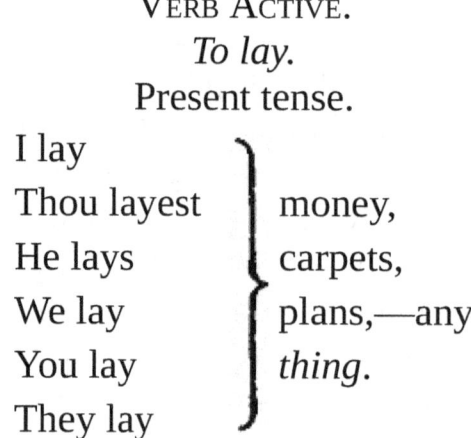

Imperfect tense.

I laid
Thou laidest
He laid
We laid
You laid
They laid
} money, carpets, plans,—any *thing*.

Present Participle, Laying.
Perfect Participle, Laid.

VERB NEUTER.
To lie.

Present tense.

I lie
Thou liest
He lies
We lie
You lie
They lie
} down, too long, on a sofa,—any *where*.

Imperfect tense.

I lay
Thou layest
He lays
We lay
You lay
They lay
} down, too long, on a sofa,—any *where*.

Present Participle, Lying,
Perfect Participle, Lain.

In such sentences as these, wherein the verb is used reflectively,—"If I lay myself down on the grass I shall catch cold," "He laid himself down on the green sward,"—the verb "to lay" is with propriety substituted for the verb "to lie;" for the addition of the emphatic pronoun *myself,* or *himself,* constituting an objective case, and coming *immediately after* the verb, *without the intervention of a preposition,* renders it necessary that the verb employed should be *active,* not *neuter,* because "active verbs govern the objective case." But this is the only construction in which "to lay" instead of "to lie" can be sanctioned by the rules of grammar.

XI.

The same confusion often arises in the use of the verbs *sit* and *set, rise* and *raise. Sit* is a neuter verb, *set* an active one; yet how often do people most improperly say, "I have *set* with him for hours," "He *set* on the beach till the sun went down," "She *set* three nights by the patient's bedside." What did they set,—potatoes, traps, or what? for as an objective case is evidently implied by the use of an active verb, an object is indispensable to complete the sense. No tense whatever of the verb "to sit" is rendered "set," which has but *one word* throughout the whole verb, except the active participle "setting;" and "sit" has but two words, "sit" and "sat," except the active participle "sitting;" therefore it is very easy to correct this error by the help of a little attention.

XII.

Raise is the same kind of verb as *set,*—active-transitive, requiring an objective case after it; and it contains only two words, *raise* and *raised,* besides the active participle *raising. Rise* is a neuter verb, not admitting an objective case. It contains two words, *rise* and *rose;* besides the two participles, *rising* and *risen.* It is improper, therefore, to say, "He *rose* the books from the floor," "He *rises* the fruit as it falls," "After she had *risen* the basket on her head," &c. In all such cases use the other verb *raise.* It occurs to me, that if people would take the trouble to reckon how many different words a verb contains, they would be in less danger of mistaking them. "Lay" contains two words, "lay" and "laid," besides the active participle "laying." "Lie" has also two words, "lie" and "lay," besides the two participles "lying" and "lain;" and from this second word "lay" arises all the confusion I have had to lament in the foregoing pages.

XIII.

To the scholar I would remark the prevalent impropriety of adopting the subjunctive instead of the indicative mood, in sentences where doubt or uncertainty is expressed, although the former can only be used in situations in which "contingency and futurity" are combined. Thus, a gentleman, giving an order to his tailor, may say, "Make me a coat of a certain description, if it *fit* me well I will give you another order;" because the "fit" alluded to is a thing which the future has to determine. But when the coat is made and brought home, he cannot say, "If this cloth *be good* I will give you another order," for the quality of the cloth is *already* determined; the future will not alter it. It may be good, it may be bad, but whatever it *may be* it already *is;* therefore, as contingency only is implied, *without futurity*, it must be rendered in the indicative mood, "If this cloth *is* good," &c. We may with propriety say, "If the book be sent in time, I shall be able to read it to-night," because the sending of the book is an event which the *future* must produce; but we must not say, "If this book be sent for me, it is a mistake," because here the act alluded to is already performed,—the book has come. I think it very likely that people have been beguiled into this error by the prefix of the conjunction, forgetting that conjunctions may be used with the indicative as well as with the subjunctive mood.

XIV.

Some people use the imperfect tense of the verb "to go," instead of the past participle, and say, "I should have *went*," instead of "I should have gone." This is *not* a very common error, but it is a very great one; and I should not have thought it could come within the range of the class for which this book is written, but that I have heard the fault committed by people of even tolerable education. One might as well say, "I should have *was* at the theatre last night," instead of "I should have *been* at the theatre," &c., as say, "I should have *went*" instead of "I should have *gone*."

XV.

Others there are who invert this error, and use the past participle of the verb "to do" instead of a tense of the verb, saying, "I *done*" instead of "I *did*." This is inadmissible. "I *did* it," or "I *have done* it," is a phrase correct in its formation, its application being, of course, dependent on other circumstances.

XVI.

There are speakers who are *too refined* to use the past (or perfect) participle of the verbs "to drink," "to run," "to begin," &c., and substitute the *imperfect tense*, as in the verb "to go." Thus, instead of saying, "I have drunk," "he has run," "they have begun," they say, "I have *drank*" "he has *ran*," "they have *began*" &c. These are minor errors, I admit; still, nice ears detect them.

XVII.

I trust it is unnecessary to warn any of my readers against adopting the flagrant vulgarity of saying "*don't* ought," and "*hadn't* ought," instead of "ought *not*." It is also incorrect to employ *no* for *not* in such phrases as, "If it is true or *no* (not)," "Is it so or *no* (not)?"

XVIII.

Many people have an odd way of saying, "I expect," when they only mean "I think," or "I conclude;" as, "I expect my brother is gone to Richmond to-day," "I expect those books were sent to Paris last year." This is wrong. *Expect* can relate only to *future* time, and must be followed by a future tense, or a verb in the infinitive mood; as, "I expect my brother *will go* to Richmond to-day," "I expect *to find* those books were sent to Paris last year." Here the introduction of a future tense, or of a verb in the infinitive mood, rectifies the grammar without altering the sense; but such a portion of the sentence must not be omitted in expression, as no such ellipsis is allowable.

XIX.

The majority of speakers use the imperfect tense and the perfect tense together, in such sentences as the following,—"I intended to *have called* on him last night," "I meant to *have purchased* one yesterday,"—or a pluperfect tense, and a perfect tense together I have sometimes heard, as, "You should *have written* to *have told* her." These expressions are illogical, because, as the *intention* to perform an act *must* be *prior* to the act contemplated, the act itself cannot with propriety be expressed by a tense indicating a period of time *previous* to the intention. The three sentences should be corrected thus, placing the second verb in the infinitive mood, "I intended *to call* on him last night," "I meant *to purchase* one yesterday," "You should have written *to tell* her."

But the imperfect tense and the perfect tense are to be combined in such sentences as the following, "I remarked that they appeared to have undergone great fatigue;" because here the act of "undergoing fatigue" *must* have taken place *previous* to the period in which you have had the opportunity of remarking its effect on their appearance; the sentence, therefore, is both grammatical and logical.

XX.

Another strange perversion of grammatical propriety is to be heard occasionally in the adoption of the present tense of the verb "to have," most probably instead of the past participle, but in situations in which the participle itself would be a redundance; such as, "If I had *have* known," "If he had *have* come according to appointment," "If you had *have* sent me that intelligence," &c. Of what utility is the word "have" in the sentence at all? What office does it perform? If it stands in place of any other word, that other word would still be an incumbrance; but the sentence being complete without it, it becomes an illiterate superfluity. "If I had *have* known that you would have been there before me, I would have written to you to *have* waited till I had *have* come." What a construction from the lips of an educated person! and yet we do sometimes hear this *slip-slop* uttered by people who are considered to "speak French and Italian *well*," and who enjoy the reputation of being "accomplished!"

XXI.

It is amusing to observe the broad line of demarcation which exists between *vulgar* bad grammar and *genteel* bad grammar, and which characterizes the violation of almost every rule of syntax. The vulgar speaker uses adjectives instead of adverbs, and says, "This letter is written *shocking;*" the genteel speaker uses adverbs instead of adjectives, and says, "This writing looks *shockingly*." The perpetrators of the latter offence may fancy they can shield themselves behind the grammatical law which compels the employment of an adverb, not an adjective, to qualify a verb, and behind the first rule of syntax, which says "a verb must agree with its nominative." But which *is* the nominative in the expression alluded to? *Which* performs the act of looking,—the writing or the speaker? To say that a thing *looks* when *we* look *at* it, is an idiom peculiar to our language, and some idioms are not reducible to rules; they are conventional terms which pass current, like bank notes, for the sterling they represent, but must not be submitted to the test of grammatical alchymy. It is improper, therefore, to say, "The queen looks beautifully," "The flowers smell sweetly," "This writing looks shockingly;" because it is the speaker that performs the act of looking, smelling, &c., not the noun looked *at;* and though, by an idiomatical construction necessary to avoid circumlocution, the sentence *imputes the act* to the *thing beheld,* the qualifying word must express the quality of the thing spoken of, *adjectively,* instead of qualifying the act of the nominative understood, *adverbially*. What an adjective is to a noun, an adverb is to a verb; an adjective expresses the quality of a thing, and an adverb the manner of an action. Consider what it is you wish to express, the *quality of a thing,* or the *manner of an action,* and use an adjective or adverb accordingly. But beware that you discriminate justly; for though you cannot say, "The queen looked *majestically* in her robes," because here the act of *looking* is performed by the spectator, who looks *at* her, you can and *must* say, "The queen looked *graciously* on the petitioner," "The queen looked *mercifully* on his prayer," because here the *act* of *looking* is performed *by* the queen. You cannot say, "These flowers smell sweetly," because it is *you* that smell, and not the flowers; but you can say, "These flowers perfume the air deliciously," because it is *they* which impart the fragrance, not you. You cannot say, "This dress looks badly," because it is you that look, not the dress; but you can say, "This dress *fits* badly," because it is the dress that performs the act of fitting either well or ill. There are some peculiar idioms which it would be better to avoid altogether, if possible; but if you feel compelled to use them, take them as they are,—you cannot prune and refine them by the rules of syntax, and to attempt to do so shows ignorance as well as affectation.

XXII.

There is a mistake often committed in the use of the adverbs of place, *hence, thence, whence.* People are apt to say, "He will go *from thence* to-morrow," &c. The preposition "from" is included in these adverbs, therefore it becomes tautology in sense when prefixed to them.

XXIII.

"Equally as well" is a very common expression, and a very incorrect one; the adverb of comparison, "as," has no right in the sentence. "Equally well," "Equally high," "Equally dear," should be the construction; and if a complement be necessary in the phrase, it should be preceded by the preposition "with," as, "The wall was equally high with the former one," "The goods at Smith's are equally dear with those sold at the shop next door," &c. "Equally the same" is tautology.

XXIV.

"Whether," sometimes an adverb, sometimes a conjunction, is a word that plainly indicates a choice of things (of course I cannot be supposed to mean a *freedom* of choice); it is highly improper, therefore, to place it, as many do, at the head of each part of a sentence, as, "I have not yet made up my mind whether I shall go to France, or *whether* I shall remain in England." The conjunction should not be repeated, as it is evident the alternative is expressed *only in the combination* of the *two* parts of the sentence, not in either of them taken separately; and the phrase should stand thus, "I have not yet made up my mind whether I shall go to France *or* remain in England."

XXV.

There is an awkwardness prevalent amongst all classes of society in such sentences as the following: "He quitted his horse, and got *on to* a stage coach," "He jumped *on to* the floor," "She laid it *on to* a dish," "I threw it *on to* the fire." Why use two prepositions where one would be quite as explicit, and far more elegant? Nobody, at the present day, would think of saying, "He came up to London *for* to go to the exhibition," because the preposition "for" would be an awkward superfluity. So is "to" in the examples given; in each of which there is an unwieldiness of construction which reminds one of the process of glueing, or fastening, one thing "on to" another. Expunge the redundant preposition, and be assured, gentle reader, the sentence will still be found "an elegant sufficiency." There are some situations, however, in which the two prepositions may with propriety be employed, though they are never indispensable, as, "I accompanied such a one to Islington, and then walked on to Kingsland." But here *two* motions are implied, the walking onward, and the reaching of a certain point. More might be said to illustrate the distinction, but we believe it will not be deemed necessary.

XXVI.

There seems to be a natural tendency to deal in a redundance of prepositions. Many people talk of "continuing *on*." I should be glad to be informed in what other direction it would be possible to *continue*.

XXVII.

It is most illiterate to put the preposition *of* after the adverb *off*, as, "The satin measured twelve yards before I cut this piece *off of* it," "The fruit was gathered *off of* that tree." Many of my readers will consider such a remark quite unnecessary in this volume; but many others, who ought to know better, must stand self-condemned on reading it.

XXVIII.

There is a false taste extant for the preposition "on" instead of "*of*" in songs, poetry, and many other situations in which there is still less excuse for borrowing the poetic license; such as, "Wilt thou think *on* me, love?" "I will think *on* thee, love," "Then think *on* the friend who once welcomed it too," &c., &c. But this is an error chiefly to be met with among poetasters and melodramatic speakers.

XXIX.

Some people add a superfluous preposition at the end of a sentence, —"More than you think *for*." This, however, is an awkwardness rarely committed by persons of decent education.

XXX.

That "prepositions govern the objective case" is a golden rule of grammar; and if it were only *well remembered*, it would effectually correct that mistake of substituting the nominative for the objective pronoun, which has been complained of in the preceding pages. In using a relative pronoun in the objective case, it is more elegant to put the preposition before than after it, thus, "To whom was the order given?" instead of, "Whom was the order given to?" Indeed, if this practice were to be invariably adopted, it would obviate the possibility of confounding the nominative with the objective case, because no man would ever find himself able to utter such a sentence as, "To who was this proposal made?" though he might very unconsciously say, "Who was this proposal made to?" and the error would be equally flagrant in both instances.

XXXI.

There is a great inaccuracy connected with the use of the disjunctive conjunctions *or* and *nor,* which seem to be either not clearly understood, or treated with undue contempt by persons who speak in the following manner: "Henry or John *are* to go there to-night," "His son or his nephew *have* since put in *their* claim," "Neither one *nor* the other *have* the least chance of success." The conjunctions disjunctive "or" and "nor" separate the objects in sense, as the conjunction copulative unites them; and as, by the use of the former, the things stand forth separately and singly to the comprehension, the verb or pronoun must be rendered in the singular number also; as, "Henry *or* John *is* to go there to-night," "His son *or* his nephew *has* since put in *his* claim," &c. If you look over the sentence, you will perceive that only *one* is to do the act, therefore only *one* can be the nominative to the verb.

XXXII.

Many people improperly substitute the disjunctive "but" for the comparative "than," as, "The mind no sooner entertains any proposition, *but* it presently hastens to some hypothesis to bottom it on."—*Locke.* "No other resource *but* this was allowed him." "My behavior," says she, "has, I fear, been the death of a man who had no other fault *but* that of loving me too much."—*Spectator.*

XXXIII.

Sometimes a relative pronoun is used instead of a conjunction, in such sentences as the following: "I don't know but *what* I shall go to Brighton to-morrow," instead of, "I don't know but *that,*" &c.

XXXIV.

Sometimes the disjunctive *but* is substituted for the conjunction *that*, as, "I have no doubt *but* he will be here to-night." Sometimes for the conjunction *if*, as, "I shouldn't wonder *but* that was the case." And sometimes *two* conjunctions are used instead of one, as, "*If that* I have offended him," "*After that* he had seen the parties," &c. All this is very awkward indeed, and ought to be avoided, and might easily be so by a little attention.

CHAPTER II.

I.

It is obsolete now to use the article *an* before words beginning with long *u* or with *eu*, and it has become more elegant, in modern style, to say, "a university," "a useful article," "a European," "a euphonious combination of sentences," &c., &c. It is also proper to say "such a one," not "such an one."

II.

Some people pronounce the plural of handkerchief, scarf, wharf, dwarf, *handkerchieves, scarves, wharves, dwarves*. This is an error, as these words, and perhaps a few others, are exceptions to the rule laid down, that nouns ending in *f* and *fe* shall change these terminations into *ves* to form the plural.

III.

There is an illiterate mode of pronouncing the adverb *too*, which is that of contracting it into the sound of the preposition *to;* thus, "I think I paid *to much* for this gun," "This line is *to long* by half." The adverb *too* should be pronounced like the numeral adjective *two*, and have the same full distinct sound in delivery, as, "I think I paid *two* much for this gun," "This line is *two* long by half."

IV.

One does not expect to hear such words as "necessi'ated," "preventative," &c., from people who profess to be educated; but one *does* hear them, nevertheless, and many others of the same genus, of which the following list is a specimen, not a collection.

"Febuary" and "Febbiwerry," instead of February.

"Seckaterry"	instead of	secretary.
"Gover'ment"	"	government.
"Eve'min"	"	evening.
"Sev'm"	"	seven.
"Holladiz"	"	holidays.
"Mossle"	"	morsel.

"Chapped," according to orthography, instead of *chopped*, according to polite usage.

And we have even heard "continental" pronounced *continential*, though upon what authority we know not. Besides these, a multitude of others might be quoted, which we consider too familiar to particularize and "too numerous to mention."

V.

There is an old jest on record of a person hearing another pronounce the word curiosity "*curosity*," and remarking to a bystander, "That man murders the English language." "Nay," replies the person addressed, "he only knocks an eye (i) out." And I am invariably reminded of this old jest whenever I hear such pronunciations as the following,—"Lat'n" for Latin, "sat'n" for satin, and Britain pronounced so as to rhyme with *written*,—of which a few examples will be given on a subsequent page, not with the wild hope of comprising in so short a space *all* the perversions of prosody which are constantly taking place, but simply with the intention of reminding careless speakers of some general principles they seem to have forgotten, and of the vast accumulation of error they may engraft upon themselves by a lazy adherence to the custom of the crowd. Before, however, proceeding to the words in question, it may be satisfactory to our readers to recall to their memory the observations of Lindley Murray on the subject. He says, "There is scarcely anything which more distinguishes a person of poor education from a person of a good one than the pronunciation of the *unaccented vowels*. When vowels are *under the accent*, the best speakers, and the lowest of the people, with very few exceptions, pronounce them in the same manner; but the *un*accented vowels in the mouths of the former have a distinct, open, and specific sound, while the latter often totally sink them, or change them into some other sound." The words that have chiefly struck me are the following, in which not only the i but some of the other vowels are submitted to the mutilating process, or, as I have heard it pronounced, *mutulating*.

Brit'n	instead of	Britain.
Lat'n	"	Latin.
Sat'n	"	Satin.
Patt'n	"	Patten.
Curt'n	"	Curtain.
Cert'n	"	Certain.
Bridle	"	Bridal.
Idle	"	Idol.
Meddle	"	Medal.
Moddle	"	Model.
Mentle	"	Mental.
Mortle	"	Mortal.
Fatle	"	Fatal.
Gravle	"	Gravel.
Travle	"	Travel.
Sudd'n	"	Sudden.
Infidle	"	Infidel.
Scroop'-lous	"	*Scru-pu*-lous.

And a long train of *et cetera*, of which the above examples do not furnish a tithe.

Note.—That to sound the e in *garden* and *often*, and the i in *evil* and *devil*, is a decided error. They should always be pronounced *gard'n* and *oft'n*, *ev'l* and *dev'l*.

Some people pronounce the *I* in Irish and its concomitants so as to make the words Ireland, Irishmen, Irish linen, &c., sound as if they were written *Arland, A-rishmen, Arish* linen, &c. This is literally "knocking an *i* out."

VI.

It is affected, and contrary to authority, to deprive the *s* of its sharp hissing sound in the words *precise, desolate, design*, and their derivatives.

VII.

There is one peculiarity which we feel bound to notice, because it has infected English speakers,—that of corrupting the *e* and the *i* into the sound of *a* or *u*, in the words ability, humility, charity, &c.; for how often is the ear wrung by such barbarisms as, humi*lutty*, civi*lutty*, qua*laty*, quan*taty*, cru*alty*, char*aty*, human*aty*, barbar*aty*, horr*uble*, terr*uble*, and so on, *ad infinitum!*—an uncouth practice, to which nothing is comparable, except pronouncing *yalla* for yellow.

VIII.

There is in some quarters a bad mode prevalent of pronouncing the plural of such words as *face, place*, &c., *fazes, plazes*, whilst the plural of *price* seems everywhere subject to the same strange mutation. The words should be *faces, places, prices*, without any softening of the *c* into *z*. There is, too, an ugly fashion of pronouncing the *ng*, when terminating a word or syllable, as *we* pronounce the same combination of letters in the word *finger*, and making such words as "singer," "ringer," &c., rhyme with *linger*. Sometimes the double *o* is elongated into the sound which we give to that dipthong in "room," "fool," "moon," &c., which has a very bad effect in such words as *book, look, nook, took*, &c.; and sometimes it is contracted into the sound of short *u*, making "foot," and some other words, rhyme with *but*.

IX.

And having remarked on the *lingering* pronunciation, it is but fair to notice a defect, the reverse of this, namely, that of omitting the final *g* in such words as *saying, going, shilling*, &c., and pronouncing them "sayin," "goin," "shillin." This is so common an error that it generally escapes notice, but is a greater blemish, where we have a right to look for perfection, than the peculiarities of the provinces in those who reside there.

X.

It is also a common fault to add a gratuitous *r* to words ending with a vowel, such as Emma*r*, Louisa*r*, Julia*r*, and to make *draw, law, saw, flaw*, with all others of the same class, rhyme with *war;* to omit the *r* in such words as *corks, forks, curtains, morsel*, &c.; in the word *perhaps*, when they conscientiously *pronounce* the *h;* and sometimes in *Paris;* or to convert it into the sound of a *y* when it comes between two vowels, as in the name *Harriet,* and in the words *superior, interior,* &c., frequently pronounced *Aah-yet, su-pe-yor, in-te-yor,* &c.

XI.

There is a vicious mode of amalgamating the final *s* of a word (and sometimes the final *c*, when preceded and followed by a vowel) with the first letter of the next word, if that letter happens to be a *y*, in such a manner as to produce the sound of *sh* or of *usu* in *usual;* as, "A *nishe* young man," "What *makesh* you laugh?" "If he *offendsh* you, don't speak to him," "*Ash* you please," "Not *jush* yet," "We always *passh* your house in going to call on *Missh* Yates,—she lives near *Palash* Yard;" and so on through all the possibilities of such a combination. This is decided, unmitigated *cockneyism*, having its parallel in nothing except the broken English of the sons of Abraham; and to adopt it in conversation is certainly "not speaking like a Christian." The effect of this pronunciation on the ear is as though the mouth of the speaker were filled with froth, which impedes the utterance, and gives the semblance of a defect where nature had kindly intended perfection; but the radical cause of this, and of many other mispronunciations, is the carelessness, sometimes the ignorance, of teachers, who permit children to read and speak in a slovenly manner, without opening their teeth, or taking any pains to acquire a distinct articulation.

XII.

Whilst we are on the subject of Prosody, we must not omit to mention the vicious pronunciation occasionally given to the words *new*, *due*, *Tuesday*, *stupid*, and a few others, sometimes corrupted into *noo*, *doo*, *Toosday*, *stoopid*, &c., by way of refinement, perhaps, for lips which are too delicate to utter the clear, broad, English *u*.

XIII.

Never say "Cut it in *half*," for this you cannot do unless you could *annihilate one* half. You may "cut it in two," or "cut it in halves," or "cut it through," or "divide it," but no human ability will enable you to *cut it in half*.

XIV.

Never speak of "lots" and "loads" of things. Young men allow themselves a diffusive license of speech, and of quotation, which has introduced many words into colloquial style that do not at all tend to improve or dignify the language, and which, when heard from *ladies'* lips, become absolute vulgarisms. A young man may talk recklessly of "lots of bargains," "lots of money," "lots of fellows," "lots of fun," &c., but a lady may *not*. Man may indulge in any latitude of expression within the bounds of sense and decorum, but woman has a narrower range,—even her mirth must be subjected to rule. It may be *naïve*, but must never be grotesque. It is not that we would have *primness* in the sex, but we would have refinement. Women are the purer and the more ornamental part of life, and when *they* degenerate, the Poetry of Life is gone.

XV.

"Loads" is a word quite as objectional as "lots," unless it can be reduced to a load of *something*, such as a *ship*-load, a *wagon*-load, a *cart*-load, a *horse*-load, &c. We often hear such expressions as "loads of shops," "loads of authors," "loads of compliments;" but as shops, authors, compliments, are things not usually piled up into loads, either for ships or horses, we cannot discover the propriety of the application.

XVI.

Some people, guiltless of those absurdities, commit a great error in the use of the word *quantity*, applying it to things of *number*, as "a quantity of friends," "a quantity of ships," "a quantity of houses," &c. *Quantity* can be applied only where *bulk* is indicated, as "a quantity of land," "a quantity of timber;" but we cannot say, "a quantity of fields," "a quantity of trees," because *trees* and *fields* are specific individualities. Or we may apply it where individualities are taken in the gross, without reference to modes, as "a quantity of luggage," "a quantity of furniture;" but we cannot say "a quantity of boxes," "a quantity of chairs and tables," for the same reason which is given in the former instances. We also apply the term *quantity* to those things of number which are too minute to be taken separately, as "a quantity of beans," "a quantity of oats," &c., &c.

XVII.

Avoid favorite words and phrases; they betray a poverty of language or of imagination not creditable to a cultivated intellect. Some people are so unfortunate as to find all things *vulgar* that come "betwixt the wind and their nobility;" others find them *disgusting*. Some are always *anticipating*, others are always *appreciating*. Multitudes are *aristocratic* in all their relations, other multitudes are as *distingués*. These two words are chiefly patronized by those whose pretensions in such respects are the most questionable. To some timid spirits, born under malignant influences no doubt, most things present an *awful* appearance, even though they come in shapes so insignificant as a cold day or an aching finger. But, thanks to that happy diversity of Nature which throws light as well as shadow into the human character, there are minds of brighter vision and more cheerful temperament, who behold all things *splendid, magnificent*, down to a cup of small beer, or a half-penny orange. Some people have a grandiloquent force of expression, thereby imparting a *tremendous* or *thundering* character even to little things. This is truly carrying their conceptions into the sublime,— sometimes a step beyond.

We have, however, no intention of particularizing *all* the "pet" phrases which salute the ear; but the enumeration of a few of them may make the *candid* culprit smile, and avoid those trifling absurdities for the future.

We would, under favor, suggest to the reader the advantage of not relying too confidently on knowledge acquired by habit and example alone. There are many words in constant use which are perverted from their original meanings; and if we were to dip into some standard dictionary occasionally, search out the true meanings of words with which we have fancied ourselves acquainted, and convict ourselves of *all* the errors we have been committing in following the crowd, our surprise, perhaps, would equal that of Molière's *Bourgeois Gentilhomme* when he discovered that he had been talking *prose* for forty years.

The words *feasible, ostensible, obnoxious, apparent, obtain, refrain, domesticated,* and *centre,* are expressions which, nine times out of ten, are misapplied, besides a host of others whose propriety is never questioned, so firmly has custom riveted the bonds of ignorance.

In closing this little volume, the writer begs leave to say that the remarks offered are intended only as "Hints," which they who desire perfection may easily improve, by a little exercise of the understanding, and a reference to more extensive sources, into a competent knowledge of their own tongue; also as *warnings* to the careless, that their lapses do not pass so unobserved as they are in the habit of supposing.

Though many of the syntactical errors herein mentioned are to be found in the works of some of our best writers, they are *errors* nevertheless, and stand as blemishes upon the productions of their genius, like unsightly excrescences upon a lovely skin. Genius is above grammar, and this conviction may inspire in some bosoms an undue contempt for the latter. But grammar is a constituent part of good education, and a neglect of it *might* argue a *want* of education, which would, perhaps, be mortifying. It is an old axiom that "civility costs nothing," and surely grammatical purity need not cost *much* to people disposed to pay a little attention to it, and who have received a respectable education already. It adds a grace to eloquence, and raises the standard of language where eloquence is not.

A handsome man or handsome woman is not improved by a shabby or slatternly attire; so the best abilities are shown to a disadvantage through a style marked by illiteracies.

MISTAKES AND IMPROPRIETIES

IN SPEAKING AND WRITING CORRECTED.

1. Have you *learned* French yet? say *learnt*, as *learned* is now used only as an adjective,—as, *a learned man*. Pronounce *learned* in *two* syllables.

2. The business would suit any one who *enjoys bad health* [from an advertisement in a London newspaper]; say, any one *in a delicate state of health*, or, *whose health is but indifferent*.

3. "We have no *corporeal* punishment here," said a schoolmaster once to the author of this little work. *Corporeal* is opposed to *spiritual;* say, *corporal* punishment. *Corporeal* means *having a body*. The Almighty is not a *corporeal* being, but a *spirit*, as St. John tells us.

4. That was a *notable* circumstance. Pronounce the first syllable of *notable* as *no* in *notion*. Mrs. Johnson is a *notable* housewife; that is to say, *careful*. Pronounce the first syllable of *notable* as *not* in *Nottingham*.

5. Put an *advertisement* in the "Times." Pronounce *advertisement* with the accent on *ver*, and not on *tise*.

6. He *rose up* and left the room; leave out *up*.

7. You have *sown* it very badly; say, *sewed* it.

8. Mr. Dupont *learnt* me French; say, *taught*. The *master teaches*, but the *pupil learns*.

9. John and Henry both read well, but John is the *best* reader; say, the *better* reader, as *best* can only be said when *three or more persons* or objects are compared.

10. The *two first* pupils I had; say, the *first two*.

11. He has *mistook* his true interest; say, *mistaken*.

12. Have you *lit* the fire, Mary? say, *lighted*.

13. The doctor *has not yet came;* say, *has not yet come.*

14. I have always *gave* him good advice; say, *given.*

15. To be is an *auxiliary* verb. Pronounce *auxiliary* in *five* syllables, sounding the second *i*, and *not in four*, as we so frequently hear it.

16. *Celery* is a pleasant edible; pronounce *celery* as it is written, and *not salary*.

17. Are you at *leisure?* pronounce *lei* in *leisure* the same as *Lei* in *Leith*, and *not* so as to rhyme with *measure.*

18. Have you seen *the Miss Browns* lately? say, *the Misses Brown.*

19. You have soon *forgot* my kindness; say, *forgotten.*

20. He keeps *his coach;* say, *his carriage.*

21. John is my *oldest* brother; say, *eldest. Elder* and *eldest* are applied to *persons,—older* and *oldest* to *things.*

22. Disputes have frequently *arose* on that subject; say, *arisen.*

23. The cloth was *wove* in a very short time; say, *woven.*

24. French is *spoke* in every state in Europe; say, *spoken.*

25. He writes as the best authors would have *wrote*, had they *writ* on the same subject; say, would have *written,*—had they *written.*

26. I prefer the *yolk* of an egg to the white; say, *yelk*, and sound the *l.*

27. He is now very *decrepid;* say, *decrepit.*

28. I am very fond of *sparrowgrass;* say, *asparagus*, and pronounce it with the accent on *par*.

29. You are very *mischievous*. Pronounce *mischievous* with the accent on *mis*, and *not on chie*, and do not say *mischievious*.

30. It was very *acceptable*. Pronounce *acceptable* with the accent on *cept*, and *not on ac,* as we so often hear it.

31. "No conversation be permitted in the Reading Room to the interruption of the company present. *Neither Smoking or Refreshments allowed*" [from the prospectus of a "Literary and Scientific Institution"]; insert *can* after *conversation*, and say, *neither smoking nor refreshments*.

32. *No extras or vacations* [from the prospectus of a schoolmistress near London]; say, *neither extras nor vacations*.

33. He is very covetous. Pronounce *covetous* as if it were written *covet us*, and *not covetyus*, as is almost universally the case.

34. I intend to *summons* him; say, *summon*. *Summons* is a *noun, and not a verb*.

35. Dearly *beloved* brethren. Pronounce *beloved* in *three* syllables, and *never in two*, as some clergymen do.

36. He is now *forsook* by every one; say, *forsaken*.

37. Not *as I know*; say, *that I know*.

38. He came *for to do* it; leave out *for*.

39. They have just *rose* from the table; say, *risen*.

40. He is quite *as good as me*; say, *as good as I*.

41. *Many an one* has done the same; say, *many a one. A*, and *not an*, is used before the *long sound of u*, that is to say, when *u* forms *a distinct syllable of itself*, as, *a unit, union, a university*. It is also used before *eu*, as, *a euphony*; and likewise before the word *ewe*, as, *a ewe*. We should also say, *a youth*, not *an youth*.

42. *Many people* think so; say, *many persons*, as *people* means *a nation*.

43. "When our ships sail among the *people* of the Eastern islands, *those people* do not ask for gold,—'iron! iron!' is the call." [From a work by a peer of literary celebrity.] Say, among the *inhabitants*; and, instead of *those people*, which is ungrammatical, say, *those persons*.

44. *Was you* reading just now? say, *were you*.

45. I have *not had no dinner yet;* say, *I have had no dinner yet*, or, *I have not yet had my dinner*, or, *any dinner*.

46. She will *never be no taller;* say, she will *never be taller*, or, she will *never be any taller*.

47. I *see him* last Monday; say, *saw him*.

48. He was *averse from* such a proceeding; say, *averse to*.

49. He has *wore* his boots three months; say, *worn*.

50. He has *trod* on my toes; say, *trodden*.

51. Have you *shook* the cloth? say, *shaken*.

52. I have *rang* several times; say, *rung*.

53. I *knowed* him at once; say, *knew*.

54. He has *growed* very much; say, *grown*.

55. George has *fell* down stairs; say, *fallen*.

56. He has *chose* a very poor pattern; say, *chosen*.

57. They have *broke* a window; say, *broken*.

58. Give me *them books;* say, *those books*.

59. My brother gave me *them there pictures;* say, gave me *those pictures*.

60. Whose are *these here books?* say, *these books*.

61. The men *which* we saw; say, *whom*.

62. The books *what* you have; say, *which*, or *that*.

63. The boy *as is* reading; say, *who is* reading.

64. The pond is *froze;* say, *frozen*.

65. He has *took* my slate; say, *taken*.

66. He has often *stole* money from him; say, *stolen*.

67. They have *drove* very fast; say, *driven*.

68. I have *rode* many miles to-day; say, *ridden*.

69. You cannot *catch* him; pronounce *catch* so as to rhyme with *match*, and not *ketch*.

70. Who has *got* my slate? leave out *got*.

71. What are you *doing of?* leave out *of*.

72. *If I was rich* I would buy a carriage; say, *If I were*.

73. We have all within us an *impetus* to sin; pronounce *impetus* with the accent on *im*, and not on *pe*, as is very often the case.

74. He may go to the *antipodes* for what I care; pronounce *antipodes* with the accent on *tip*, and let *des* rhyme with *ease*. It is a word of *four* syllables, and *not of three*, as many persons make it.

75. *Vouchsafe*, a word seldom used, but, when used, the first syllable should rhyme with *pouch. Never say, vousafe*.

76. Ginger is a good *stomachic;* pronounce *stomachic* with the accent on *mach*, sounding this syllable *mak*, and *not mat*, as is often the case.

77. The land in those parts is very *fertile;* pronounce *fertile* so as to rhyme with *pill*. The *ile* in all words must be sounded *ill*, with the exception of *exile, senile, gentile, reconcile,* and *camomile,* in which *ile* rhymes with *mile*.

78. *It is surprising the fatigue he undergoes;* say, *The fatigue he undergoes is surprising*.

79. *Benefited;* often spelt *benefitted,* but *incorrectly*.

80. *Gather* up the fragments; pronounce *gather* so as to rhyme with *lather*, and *not gether*.

81. I *propose* going to town next week; say, *purpose*.

82. If I *am not mistaken,* you are in the wrong; say, If I *mistake not.*

83. *Direct* your letters to me at Mr. Jones's; say, *Address* your letters.

84. Wales is a very *mountainious* country; say, *mountainous*, and place the accent on *moun*.

85. Of two evils choose *the least;* say, *the less.*

86. *Exag'gerate;* pronounce *exad'gerate,* and *do not sound agger* as in the word *dagger,* which is a very common mistake.

87. He knows *little or nothing of Latin;* say, *little, if anything, of Latin.*

88. He keeps a *chaise;* pronounce it *shaise,* and not *shay.* It has a regular plural, *chaises.*

88. The *drought* lasted a long time; pronounce *drought* so as to rhyme with *snout,* and not *drowth.*

90. The man was *hung* last week; say, *hanged;* but say, I am fond of *hung beef. Hang, to take away life by hanging,* is a regular verb.

91. We *conversed together* on the subject; leave out *together,* as it is implied in *conversed, con* being equivalent to *with,* that is to say, We talked *with each other,* &c.

92. The affair was *compromised;* pronounce *compromised* in three syllables, and place the accent on *com,* sounding *mised* like *prized.* The word has nothing to do with *promised.* The noun *compromise* is accented like *compromised,* but *mise* must be pronounced *mice.*

93. A *steam-engine;* pronounce *engine* with *en* as in *pen,* and *not like in,* and *gine* like *gin.*

94. Numbers were *massacred;* pronounce *massacred* with the accent on *mas,* and *red* like *erd,* as if *mas'saker'd,* never *mas'sacreed.*

95. The king of Israel and the king of Judah sat *either of them* on his throne; say, *each of them. Either* signifies the *one* or the *other,* but *not both. Each* relates to *two or more objects,* and signifies *both of the two,* or *every*

one of any number taken singly. Never say "either of the three," but "*each* or *any one* of the three."

96. A *respite* was granted the convict; pronounce *respite* with the accent on *res*, and sound *pite* as *pit*.

97. He soon *returned back;* leave out *back*, which is implied by *re* in *returned*.

98. The *horizon* is the line that terminates the view; pronounce *horizon* with the accent on *ri*, and not on *ho*.

99. She has *sang* remarkably well; say, *sung*.

100. He had *sank* before assistance arrived; say, *sunk*.

101. I have often *swam* across the Tyne; say, *swum*.

102. I found my friend better than I expected *to have found him;* say, *to find him*.

103. I intended *to have written* a letter yesterday; say, *to write,* as however long it now is since I thought of writing, "*to write*" was then present to me, and must still be considered as present when I bring back that time and the thoughts of it.

104. His death *shall be* long regretted [from a notice of a death in a newspaper]; say, *will be* long, &c. *Shall* and *will* are often confounded; the following rule, however, may be of use to the reader. Mere *futurity* is expressed by *shall* in the *first* person, and by *will* in the *second* and *third;* the *determination* of the speaker by *will* in the *first,* and *shall* in the *second* and *third;* as, I WILL go to-morrow, I SHALL go to-morrow. N. B. The latter sentence simply expresses a future event; the former expresses my determination.

105. "*Without* the grammatical form of a word can be recognized at a glance, little progress can be made in reading the language" [from a very popular work on the study of the Latin language]; say, *Unless* the grammatical, &c. The use of *without* for *unless* is a very common mistake.

106. Have you begun *substraction* yet? say, *subtraction*.

107. He claimed admission to the *chiefest* offices; say, *chief*. *Chief, right, supreme, correct, true, universal, perfect, consummate, extreme*, &c., imply the superlative degree without *est* or *most*. In language sublime or impassioned, however, the word *perfect* requires the superlative form to give it effect. A lover, enraptured with his mistress, would naturally call her the *most perfect* of her sex.

108. The ship had *sprang* a leak; say, *sprung*.

109. I *had rather* do it now; say, I *would rather*.

110. He was served with a *subpœna;* pronounce *subpœna* with the accent on *pœ*, which you will sound like *tea*, and sound the *b* distinctly. *Never pronounce the word soopee'na.*

111. I have not travelled *this twenty years;* say, *these twenty years.*

112. He is *very much the gentleman;* say, He is *a very gentlemanly man*, or *fellow*.

113. The *yellow* part of an egg is very nourishing; *never* pronounce *yellow* like *tallow*, which we so often hear.

114. We are going to the *zoological* gardens; pronounce *zoological* in *five* syllables, and place the accent on *log* in *logical*. Sound *log* like *lodge*, and *the first two o's in distinct syllables. Never* make *zool one* syllable.

115. He always preaches *extempore;* pronounce *extempore* in *four* syllables, with the accent on *tem*, and *never in three*, making *pore* to rhyme with *sore*.

116. *Naught* and *aught; never* spell these words *nought* and *ought*. There is no such word as *nought*, and *ought* is a verb.

117. Allow me to *suggest;* pronounce *sug* so as to rhyme with *mug*, and *gest* like *jest*. Never *sudjest*.

118. The Emperor of Russia is a *formidable* personage; pronounce *formidable* with the accent on *for*, and *not on mid*, as is often the case.

119. Before the words *heir, herb, honest, honor, hostler, hour, humble,* and *humor,* and their compounds, instead of the article *a*, we make use of *an*, as the *h* is not sounded; likewise before words beginning with *h* that are *not* accented on the *first syllable*, such as *heroic, historical, hypothesis,* &c., as, *an heroic action, an historical work, an hypothesis* that can scarcely be allowed. N. B. The letter *h* is seldom mute at the beginning of a word; but from the negligence of tutors and the inattention of pupils many persons have become almost incapable of acquiring its just and full pronunciation. It is, therefore, incumbent on teachers to be particularly careful to inculcate a clear and distinct utterance of this sound.

120. He was *such an extravagant young man* that he soon spent his whole patrimony; say, *so extravagant a young man.*

121. I saw the *slough* of a snake; pronounce *slough* so as to rhyme with *rough.*

122. She is *quite the lady;* say, She is *very lady-like in her demeanor.*

123. He is *seldom or ever* out of town; say, *seldom, if ever,* out of town.

124. Death *unloosed* his chains; say, *loosed* his chains.

125. It is dangerous to walk *of a* slippery morning; say, *on a* slippery morning.

126. He who makes himself famous by his eloquence, illustrates his origin, let it be *never so mean;* say, *ever so mean.*

127. His fame is acknowledged *through* Europe; say, *throughout* Europe.

128. The bank of the river is frequently *overflown;* say, *overflowed.*

129. *Previous to* my leaving England I called on his lordship; say, *previously to* my leaving, &c.

130. I doubt *if this* will ever reach you; say, *whether this,* &c.

131. He was *exceeding kind* to me; say, *exceedingly kind.*

132. I lost *near* twenty pounds; say, *nearly.*

133. *Bills are requested to be paid quarterly;* say, *It is requested that bills be paid quarterly.*

134. It was *no use asking* him any more questions; say, *of no use to ask him,* &c.

135. The Americans said they *had no right* to pay taxes; say, they *were under no obligation* to pay, &c.

136. I *throwed* my box away, and *never took no more snuff;* say, I *threw,* &c., and *took snuff no more.*

137. She was *endowed* with an exquisite taste for music; say, *endued* with, &c.

138. I intend to *stop* at home; say, to *stay.*

139. At this time I *grew* my own corn; say, I *raised,* &c.

140. He *was* no sooner departed than they expelled his officers; say, he *had* no sooner, &c.

141. He *was* now retired from public business; say, *had* now retired, &c.

142. They *were* embarked in a common cause; say, *had* embarked, &c.

143. Hostilities *were* now become habitual; say, *had* now become.

144. Brutus and Aruns killed *one another;* say, *each other.*

145. Pray, sir, who *may you be?* say, who *are you?*

146. Their character as a warlike people *is* much degenerated; say, *has* much, &c.

147. He is gone on an *errand;* pronounce *errand* as it is written, and not *arrant.*

148. In a popular work on arithmetic we find the following sum,—"If for 7*s.* 8*d.*, I can buy 9 lbs. of raisins, *how much* can I purchase for £56 16*s.*?" say, "*what quantity* can I," &c. Who would think of saying "*how much raisins?*"

149. Be very careful in distinguishing between *indite* and *indict; key* and *quay; principle* and *principal; check* and *cheque; marshal* and *martial; counsel* and *council; counsellor* and *councillor; fort* and *forte; draft* and *draught; place* and *plaice; stake* and *steak; satire* and *satyr; stationery* and *stationary; ton* and *tun; levy* and *levee; foment* and *ferment; fomentation* and *fermentation; petition* and *partition; practice* and *practise; Francis* and *Frances; dose* and *doze; diverse* and *divers; device* and *devise; wary* and *weary; salary* and *celery; radish* and *reddish; treble* and *triple; broach* and *brooch; ingenious* and *ingenuous; prophesy* and *prophecy; fondling* and *foundling; lightning* and *lightening; genus* and *genius; desert* and *dessert; currier* and *courier; pillow* and *pillar; executer* and *executor; suit* and *suite; ridicule* and *reticule; lineament* and *liniment; track* and *tract; lickerish* and *licorice; statute* and *statue; ordinance* and *ordnance; lease* and *leash; recourse* and *resource; straight* and *strait; immerge* and *emerge; style* and *stile; compliment* and *complement; bass* and *base; contagious* and *contiguous; eminent* and *imminent; eruption* and *irruption; precedent* and *president; relic* and *relict*.

150. I prefer *radishes* to *cucumbers;* pronounce *radishes* exactly as it is spelt, and not *redishes*, and the *u* in the first syllable of *cucumber* as in *fuel*, and not as if the word were *cowcumber*.

151. Never pronounce *barbarous* and *grievous, bartarious* and *grievious*.

152. The *two last* chapters are very interesting; say, The *last two*, &c.

153. The soil on these islands is so very thin, that little vegetation is produced upon them *beside* cocoanut trees; say, *with the exception of*, &c.

154. He restored it *back* to the owner; leave out *back*.

155. *Here, there, where,* are generally better than *hither, thither, whither,* with verbs of motion; as, *Come here, Go there.* N. B. *Hither, thither,* and *whither,* which were formerly used, are now considered stiff and inelegant.

156. *As far as I* am able to judge, the book is well written; say, *So far as*, &c.

157. It is doubtful whether he will play *fairly or no;* say, *fairly or not*.

158. "The Pilgrim's *Progress;*" pronounce *progress, prog-ress,* not *pro-gress.*

159. He is a boy of a great *spirit;* pronounce *spirit* exactly as it is written, and never *sperit.*

160. The *camelopard* is the tallest of known animals; pronounce *camelopard* with the accent on the *second* syllable. Never call it *camel leopard,* as is so often heard.

161. He is very *awkward;* never say, *awkard.*

162. He ran *again* me; I stood *again* the wall; instead of *again,* say *against.* Do it *again* the time I mentioned; say, *by* the time, &c.

163. I always act *agreeable* to my promise; say, *agreeably.*

164. The study of syntax should be *previously* to that of punctuation; say, *previous.*

165. No one should incur censure for being tender of *their* reputation; say, of *his* reputation.

166. They were all *drownded;* say, *drowned.*

167. *Jalap* is of great service; pronounce *jalap* exactly as it is written, NEVER *jollop.*

168. He is gone on a *tour;* pronounce *tour* so as to rhyme with *poor, never* like *tower.*

169. The rain *is* ceased; say, *has* ceased.

170. *They laid their heads together,* and formed their plan; say, *They held a consultation,* &c. *Laid their heads together* savors of SLANG.

171. The *chimley* wants sweeping; say, *chimney.*

172. I was walking *towards* home; pronounce *towards* so as to rhyme with *boards. Never* say *to wards.*

173. It is a *stupenduous* work; say, *stupendous.*

174. A *courier* is expected from Paris; pronounce *cou* in *courier* so as to rhyme with *too*. *Never* pronounce *courier* like *currier*.

175. Let each of us mind *their* own business; say, *his* own business.

176. Is this or that the *best* road? say, the *better* road.

177. *Rinse* your mouth; pronounce *rinse* as it is written, and NEVER *rense*. "Wrench your mouth," said a fashionable dentist one day to the author of this work.

178. The book is not *as* well printed as it ought to be; say, *so* well printed, &c.

179. Webster's *Dictionary* is an admirable work; pronounce *dictionary* as if written *dik-shun-a-ry; not,* as is too commonly the practice, *dixonary*.

180. Some disaster has certainly *befell* him; say, *befallen*.

181. She is a pretty *creature;* never pronounce *creature, creeter,* as is often heard.

182. We went to see the *Monument;* pronounce *monument* exactly as it is written, and *not* as many pronounce it, *moniment*.

183. I am very wet, and must go and *change myself;* say, *change my clothes*.

184. He has had a good *education;* never say, *edication,* which is often heard, nor *edicate* for *educate*.

185. He is much better *than me;* say, *than I*.

186. You are stronger *than him;* say, *than he*.

187. I had *as lief* stand; say, I *would as soon* stand.

188. He is *not a whit* better; say, *in no degree* better.

189. They are *at loggerheads;* say, *at variance*.

190. His character is *undeniable,*—a very common expression; say, *unexceptionable*.

191. Bring me the *lantern;* never spell *lantern, lanthorn.*

192. The room is twelve *foot* long, and nine *foot* broad; say, twelve *feet,* nine *feet.*

193. He is *singular,* though *regular* in his habits, and also very *particular;* beware of leaving out the *u* in *singular, regular,* and *particular,* which is a very common practice.

194. They are detained *at* France; say, *in* France.

195. He lives *at* London; say, *in* London, and beware of pronouncing *London,* as many careless persons do, *Lunnun. At* should be applied to small towns.

196. No *less* than fifty persons were there; say, No *fewer,* &c.

197. *Such another* mistake, and we shall be ruined; say, Another such mistake, &c.

198. It is *some distance* from our house; say, *at some distance,* &c.

199. I shall call *upon* him; say, *on* him.

200. He is a Doctor of *Medicine;* pronounce *medicine* in *three* syllables, NEVER in *two.*

201. They told me to enter *in;* leave out *in,* as it is implied in *enter.*

202. His *strength* is amazing; never say, *strenth.*

203. "*Mistaken* souls, who dream of heaven,"—this is the beginning of a popular hymn; it should be, "*Mistaking* souls," &c. *Mistaken wretch,* for *mistaking wretch,* is an apostrophe that occurs everywhere among our poets, particularly those of the stage; the most incorrigible of all, and the most likely to fix and disseminate an error of this kind.

204. Give me both *of* those books; leave out *of.*

205. Whenever I try to write well, I *always* find I can do it; leave out *always,* which is unnecessary.

206. He plunged *down* into the stream; leave out *down*.

207. She is the *matron;* say *may-tron*, and not *mat-ron*.

208. Give me *leave* to tell you; NEVER say *leaf* for *leave*.

209. The *height* is considerable; pronounce *height* so as to rhyme with *tight*. Never *hate* nor *heighth*.

210. Who has my *scissors?* never call *scissors, sithers*.

211. First *of all* I shall give you a lesson in French, and last *of all* in music; leave out *of all* in both instances, as unnecessary.

212. I shall have finished by the *latter* end of the week; leave out *latter*, which is unnecessary.

213. They sought him *throughout* the *whole* country; leave out *whole*, which is implied in *throughout*.

214. Iron sinks *down* in water; leave out *down*.

215. I own that I did not come soon enough; but *because why?* I was detained; leave out *because*.

216. Have you seen the new *pantomime?* never say *pantomine*, as there is no such word.

217. I *cannot by no means* allow it; say, I *can by no means*, &c., or, I *cannot by any means*, &c.

218. He *covered it over;* leave out *over*.

219. I bought *a new pair of shoes;* say, *a pair of new shoes*.

220. He *combined together* these facts; leave out *together*.

221. My brother called on me, and we *both* took a walk; leave out *both*, which is unnecessary.

222. The *duke* discharged his *duty;* sound the *u* in *duke* and *duty* like the word *you*, and carefully avoid saying, *dook* and *dooty*, or *doo* for *dew*.

223. *Genealogy, geography,* and *geometry* are words of Greek derivation; beware of saying, *geneology, jography,* and *jometry,* a very common practice.

224. He made out the *inventory;* place the accent in *inventory* on the syllable *in,* and NEVER on *ven.*

225. He deserves *chastisement;* say, *chas-tiz-ment,* with the accent on *chas,* and NEVER on *tise.*

226. He threw the *rind* away; never call *rind, rine.*

227. They contributed to his *maintenance;* pronounce *maintenance* with the accent on *main,* and *never* say, *maintainance.*

228. She wears a silk *gown;* never say, *gownd.*

229. Sussex is a *maritime* county; pronounce the *last* syllable of *maritime* so as to rhyme with *rim.*

230. He *hovered* about the enemy; pronounce *hovered* so as to rhyme with *covered.*

231. He is a powerful *ally; never* place the accent on *al* in *ally,* as many do.

232. She bought a *diamond* necklace; pronounce *diamond* in *three* syllables, NEVER in *two,* which is a very common practice.

233. He reads the "Weekly *Despatch;*" NEVER spell the word *despatch, dispatch.*

234. He said *as how* you *was* to do it; say, he said *that you were to do it.*

235. Never say, "I *acquiesce with you;*" but, "I *acquiesce in your proposal, in your opinion,*" &c.

236. He is a distinguished *antiquarian;* say, *antiquary. Antiquarian* is an adjective; *antiquary,* a noun.

237. In Goldsmith's "History of England" we find the following extraordinary sentence in one of the chapters on the reign of Queen

Elizabeth:—"This" [a communication to Mary, Queen of Scots] "they effected by conveying their letters to her by means of a brewer *that supplied the family with ale through a chink in the wall of her apartment.*" A queer brewer that,—to supply his ale through a chink in the wall! How easy the alteration to make the passage clear! "This they effected by conveying their letters to her *through a chink in the wall of her apartment, by means of a brewer that supplied the family with ale.*"

238. Lavater wrote on *Physiognomy;* in the last word sound the *g* distinctly, as *g* is always pronounced before *n* when it is not in the same syllable; as, *indignity*, &c.

239. She is a very clever *girl;* pronounce *girl* as if written *gerl;* never say *gal*, which is very vulgar.

240. He built a large *granary;* pronounce *granary* so as to rhyme with *tannery*, never call the word *grainary*.

241. Beware of using *Oh!* and *O* indiscriminately; *Oh!* is used to express the emotion of *pain, sorrow,* or *surprise;* as, "Oh! the exceeding grace of God, who loves his creatures so." *O* is used to express *wishing, exclamation,* or a direct *address* to a person; as,

> "O mother, will the God above,
> Forgive my faults like thee?"

242. Some writers make a distinction between *farther* and *further;* they are, in fact, the very same word. *Further,* however, is less used than *farther,* though it is the genuine form.

243. He did it *unbeknown* to us; say, *unknown,* &c.

244. If I say "They retreated *back,*" I use a word that is *superfluous,* as *back* is implied in the syllable *re* in *retreated.* Never place the accent on *flu* in *superfluous,* but always on *per.*

245. In reading Paley's "Evidences of Christianity," I unexpectedly *lit on* the passage I wanted; say, *met with* the passage, &c.

246. He has ordered a *phaeton* from his coach-maker; beware of saying, *pheton* or *phaton.* The word should always be pronounced in *three* syllables, with the accent on *pha.* N. B. In pha-e-ton the *a* and *e* do *not* form a diphthong, as many suppose; the word is of Greek origin.

247. Be careful to use the hyphen (-) correctly; it joins compound words, and words broken by the ending of the line. The use of the hyphen will appear more clearly from the following example: "*many colored* wings" means *many* wings, which are *colored;* but "*many-colored* wings" means "wings of *many colors.*"

248. He had to wait in an *antechamber;* carefully avoid spelling the last word *antichamber.* N. B. An *antechamber* is the chamber that leads to the chief apartment. *Ante* is a Latin preposition, and means *before,* as, to ante*date,* that is, "to date beforehand." *Anti* is a Greek preposition, and means *against,* as, anti*monarchical,* that is, "against government by a single person."

249. The *axe* was very sharp; never spell *axe* without the *e.*

250. The force of voice, which is placed on any particular word or words to distinguish the sense, is called *emphasis* and those words are called *emphatical words:* as, "Grammar is a *useful* science." In this sentence the

word *useful* is emphatical. The great importance of *emphasis* may be seen by the following example:

> 1. Will you *call* on me to-morrow?
> Yes, I shall [*call*].
>
> 2. Will you call on *me* to-morrow?
> No, but I shall call on your *brother*.
>
> 3. Will you call on me *to-morrow?*
> No, but I shall on the *following day*.
>
> 4. Will *you* call on me to-morrow?
> No, but my *brother* will.

251. Never say *o-fences* for *offences; pison* for *poison; co-lection* for *collection; voiolent* for *violent; kiver* for *cover; afeard* for *afraid; debbuty* for *deputy*.

252. He is a mere *cipher;* never spell *cipher* with a *y*.

253. I was *necessitated* to do it; a vile expression, and often made worse by *necessiated* being used. Say, I was *obliged*, or *compelled*, to do it.

254. Gibbon wrote the "*Rise* and Fall of the Roman Empire;" pronounce *rise*, the noun, so as to rhyme with *price; rise*, the verb, rhymes with *prize*.

255. Have you been to the *National* Gallery? Never pronounce *national* as if it were written *nay-shun-al*, a very common error, and by no means confined to uneducated persons.

256. I bought a new *umbrella;* beware of pronouncing *umbrella, umberella*, or *umbereller*, both very common errors.

257. He is a supporter of the *government;* beware of omitting the *n* in the second syllable of *government*. A very common practice.

258. He strenuously maintained the *contrary;* never place the accent on the *second* syllable in *contrary*. In the ancient and time-honored ditty, however, of

"Mistress Mary,
Quite *contrary*,
How does your garden grow?"

a ballad with which we are all more or less familiar, the word "*contrary*" is accented on the *second* syllable, so as to rhyme with the name of the venerable dame to whom these memorable lines were addressed.

259. "Received this day *of* Mr. Brown, ten pounds;" say, "Received this day *from*", &c.

260. "In what case is the word *dominus?*" "In the *nominative*, sir." In the hurry of school pronunciation "*nominative*" is nearly always heard in *three* syllables, as if written *nomnative* or *nomative*, an error that should be very carefully avoided; it is a word of *four* syllables.

261. Of whatever you *get*, endeavor to save something; and, with all your *getting*, *get* wisdom. Carefully avoid saying *git* for *get*, and *gitting* for *getting*.

262. So intent was he on the song he was *singing*, as he stood by the fire, that he did not perceive that his clothes were *singeing*. N. B. Verbs ending with a *single e* omit the *e* when the termination *ing* is added; as, *give*, *giving*. In *singeing*, however, the *e* must be retained, to prevent its being confounded with *singing*.

263. The boy had a *swingeing* for *swinging* without permission. *Read the preceding note.*

264. The man who was *dyeing* said that his father was then *dying*. Read the note in No. 262, in reference to *dyeing;* and observe that *die* changes the *i* into *y* before the addition of the termination *ing*.

265. His *surname* is Clifford; never spell the *sur* in *surname, sir*, which shows an ignorance of is true derivation, which is from the Latin.

266. In "Bell's Life in London," of Saturday, Jan. 13th, of the current year [1855], there is a letter from a Scotchman to the editor on the subject of the declining salmon fisheries in Scotland. In one passage the writer thus expresses himself: "The Duke of Sutherland has got *almost no rent* for these

[salmon] rivers for the last four years," &c. The writer should have said, *scarcely any rent*. "*Almost no rent*" is a downright Scotticism.

267. His *mamma* sent him to a preparatory school; *mamma* is often written with one *m* only, which is not, as may at first be supposed, in imitation of the French [*maman*], but in sheer ignorance. The word is pure Greek.

268. Active verbs often take a neuter sense; as, *The house is building.* Here *is building* is used in a neuter signification, because it has no object after it. By this rule are explained such sentences as, *Application is wanting, The grammar is printing,* &c.

269. He *attackted* me without the slightest provocation; say, *attacked*.

270. I saw him *somewheres* in the city; say, *somewhere*. N. B. *Nowheres, everywheres*, and *anywheres* are also very frequently heard.

271. He is still a *bacheldor;* say, *bachelor*.

272. His language was quite *blasphemous;* beware of placing the accent on *phe* in *blasphemous*. A very common mistake. Place the accent on the syllable *blas*.

273. I fear I shall *discommode* you; say, *incommode*.

274. I can do it *equally as well as* he; leave out *equally*, which is altogether superfluous.

275. We could not forbear *from* doing it; leave out *from*, which is unnecessary.

276. They accused him *for* neglecting his duty; say, *of* neglecting, &c.

277. He was made much *on* at Bath; say, made much *of*, &c.

278. He is a man *on* whom you can confide; say, *in* whom, &c.

279. *I'm thinking* he will soon arrive; say, *I think*, &c.

280. He was obliged to *fly* the country; say, *flee* the country. A very common mistake.

281. The snuffers *wants* mending; say, *want* mending.

282. His conduct admits *of* no apology; leave out *of*, which is quite unnecessary.

283. A *gent* has been here, inquiring for you,—a detestable, but very common, expression; say, a *gentleman*, &c.

284. That was *all along of* you; say, That was *all your fault*.

285. You have no *call* to be vexed with me; say, no *occasion*, &c.

286. I *don't* know nothing about it,—a very common cockneyism; leave out *don't*.

287. I *had* rather not, should be, I *would* rather not.

288. I *had better* go, should be, *It were better* that I should go.

289. A *new pair* of gloves, should be, A *pair of new* gloves.

290. He is a *very rising* man, should be, He is *rising rapidly*.

291. Apartments *to let*, should be, Apartments *to be let*.

292. No *less* than ten persons, should be, No *fewer* than ten persons. *Less* must be applied to quantity, as, No *less* than ten pounds. *Fewer* must be applied to things.

293. I *never* speak, *whenever* I can help it, should be, I never speak *when* I can help it.

294. *Before* I do that, I must *first* be paid, should be, Before I do that, I must be paid.

295. To *get over* an illness, should be, To *survive*, or, To *recover from* an illness.

296. To *get over* a person, should be, To *persuade* a person.

297. To *get over* a fact, should be, To *deny* or *refute* it.

298. The *then* Duke of Bedford, should be, The Duke of Bedford *of that day*, or, The *sixth* Duke of Bedford.

299. The *then* Mrs. Howard, should be, The Mrs. Howard *then living*.

300. A *couple* of pounds, should be, *Two* pounds. Couple implies union, as, A married couple.

301. He speaks *slow*, should be, He speaks *slowly*.

302. He is *noways* in fault, should be, He is *nowise* in fault.

303. He is *like* to be, should be, He is *likely* to be.

304. *All over* the land, should be, *Over all* the land.

305. I am stout in comparison *to* you, should be, I am stout in comparison *with* you.

306. At *best*, should be, At *the best*.

307. At *worst*, should be, At *the worst*.

308. The dinner was *all eat up*, should be, The dinner was *all eaten*.

309. I *eat* heartily, should be, I *ate* heartily.

310. As I *take* it, should be, As I *see* it, or *understand* it.

311. I shall *fall down*, should be, I shall *fall*.

312. It fell *on* the floor, should be, It fell *to* the floor.

313. He *again repeated* it, should be, He *repeated* it.

314. His conduct was *approved of* by all, should be, His conduct was *approved* by all.

315. He was killed *by* a cannon ball, should be, He was killed *with* a cannon ball. The gun was fired *by* a man.

316. Six weeks *back*, should be, Six weeks *ago*, or *since*.

317. *Every now and then*, should be, *Often*, or *Frequently*.

318. Who finds him *in* money? should be, Who finds him money?

319. The *first of all*, should be, The *first*.

320. The *last of all*, should be, The *last*.

321. Be that as it *will*, should be, Be that as it *may*.

322. My *every* hope, should be, *All* my hopes.

323. Since *when*, should be, Since *which time*.

324. He put it *in* his pocket, should be, He put it *into* his pocket.

325. Since *then*, should be, Since *that time*.

326. The *latter* end, should be, The *end*.

327. I saw it *in here*, should be, I saw it *here*.

328. That *ay'nt* just, should be, That *is not* just.

329. The hen is *setting*, should be, The hen is *sitting*.

330. The wind *sets*, should be, The wind *sits*.

331. To *lift up*, should be, To *lift*.

332. I said so *over again*, should be, I *repeated* it.

333. From *here to there*, should be, From *this place to that*.

334. *Nobody else* but him, should be, *Nobody* but him.

335. The balloon *ascended up*, should be, The balloon *ascended*.

336. *This* two days, should be, *These* two days.

337. Do you *mean* to come? should be, Do you *intend* to come?

338. Each of them *are*, should be, Each of them *is*. *Each* means one *and* the other of two.

339. *Either* of the *three*, should be, *Any one* of the three. *Either* means one *or* the other of two.

340. *Neither* one *or* the other, should be, Neither one *nor* the other. *Neither* (not either) means not the one *nor* the other of two.

341. Better *nor* that, should be, Better *than* that.

342. *Bad grammar*, should be, Bad or ungrammatical *English*.

343. As soon as *ever*, should be, As soon as.

344. You will *some* day be sorry, should be, You will *one* day be sorry.

345. From *now*, should be, From *this time*.

346. Therefore, I *thought* it proper to write you, should be, Therefore, I *think* it proper to write *to* you.

347. *There's* thirty, should be, There *are* thirty.

348. *Subject matter*, should be, The subject.

349. A *summer's* morning, should be, A *summer* morning.

350. My clothes *have got* too small, or too short, for me, should be, I have become too stout or too tall for my clothes.

351. A *most perfect* poem, should be, A *perfect* poem. Perfect, supreme, complete, brief, full, empty, true, false, do not admit of comparison.

352. Avoid using unmeaning or vulgar phrases in speaking, as, You don't say so? Don't you know? Don't you see? You know; You see; So, you see, &c.

353. Is Mr. Smith *in?* should be, Is Mr. Smith *within?*

354. The *other one*, should be, The other.

355. *Another one*, should be, Another.

356. I *left* this morning. Name the place left.

357. Over head *and ears*, should be, Over *head*.

358. I may *perhaps*, or *probably*, should be, I may.

359. Whether he will or *no*, should be, Whether he will or *not*.

360. *Says* I, should be, *Said* I, or, I *said*.

361. He spoke *contemptibly* of him, should be, He spoke *contemptuously* of him.

362. *Was* you? should be, *Were* you?

363. I am *oftener* well than ill, should be, I am *more frequently* well than ill.

364. For *good and all*, should be, For *ever*.

365. It is *above* a month since, should be, It is *more* then a month since.

366. He is a *superior* man, should be, He is *superior to most* men.

367. He *need* not do it, should be, He *needs* not do it.

368. Go *over* the bridge, should be, Go *across* the bridge.

369. I was some distance from home, should be, I was *at* some distance from home.

370. He *belongs* to the *Mechanics'* Institution, should be, He is a *member* of the *Mechanics'* Institution.

371. For *such another* book, should be, For *another such* book.

372. They *mutually* loved *each other*, should be, They loved *each other*.

373. I *ay'nt*, should be, I *am not*.

374. I am *up to you*, should be, I *understand* you.

375. Bread has *rose*, should be, Bread has *risen*.

376. He was in *eminent* danger, should be, He was in *imminent* danger.

377. Take hold *on*, should be, Take hold *of*.

378. Vegetables were *plenty*, should be, Vegetables were *plentiful*.

379. Avoid all slang and vulgar words and phrases, as, *Any how, Bating, Bran new, To blow up, Bother, Cut, Currying favor, Fork out, Half an eye, I am up to you, Kick up, Leastwise, Nowheres, Pell-mell, Scrape, The Scratch, Rum, Topsy-turvey, Walk into, Whatsomever.*

"Be thou familiar, but by no means vulgar."—SHAKESPEARE.

www.ingramcontent.com/pod-product-compliance
Lightning Source LLC
Chambersburg PA
CBHW081729100526
44591CB00016B/2553